4 Week Loan

This book is due for return on or before the last date shown below

University of Cumbria
24/7 renewals Tel:0845 602 6124

Sophia Loren
Moulding the Star

Pauline Small

intellect Bristol, UK / Chicago, USA

First published in the UK in 2009 by
Intellect Books, The Mill, Parnall Road, Fishponds, Bristol, BS16 3JG, UK

First published in the USA in 2009 by
Intellect Books, The University of Chicago Press, 1427 E. 60th Street, Chicago,
IL 60637, USA

A catalogue record for this book is available from the British Library.

Cover designer: Holly Rose
Copy-editor: Rebecca Vaughn-Williams
Typesetting: Mac Style, Beverley, E. Yorkshire

ISBN 978-1-84150-234-2

Printed and bound by Gutenberg Press, Malta.

CONTENTS

ACKNOWLEDGEMENTS

I have been assisted in writing this book in a number of ways. I acknowledge the financial support of the British Academy, the University of London Central Research Fund, the School of Languages, Linguistics and Film and the Film Department of Queen Mary University of London. My research was greatly facilitated by the expertise of Sean Delaney and all the staff of the British Film Institute Library in London, Elisabetta Chiarotti of the Cineteca Nazionale in Rome, and the staff of the Archivio Centrale dello Stato in Rome. I am most grateful to Mary Wood, Brian Richardson, Chris Wagstaff, Adalgisa Giorgio and Judith Bryce for their support and advice on my work, and my colleagues at Queen Mary, with whom it is such a pleasure to work. I wish to thank specifically Peter Evans, for reading and suggesting amendments to preliminary drafts of the manuscript; Mina Fabbri, for giving me access to her superb private collection of Sophia Loren materials, and for the warm hospitality she and her family gave me in their home; Pier Luigi Raffaelli, who patiently initiated me into the labyrinth of Italian government film archives; and to my family, for living with me (and Sophia) through the long period of preparing and writing the book. Without them, it would never have been completed successfully. Thanks are also due to Intellect Books who took on the publishing of this project and brought it to fruition. Naturally, any errors the book contains are mine alone.

NOTE: 'Sophia' or 'Sofia'? As explained in Chapter Two, Sofia Scicolone at first took the professional name Sofia Lazzaro, then changed it again, still at an early stage in her career, to Sophia Loren. In general Italian contributors, including De Sica, Giuseppe Marotta and Gian Luigi Rondi, repeatedly persist in using the form 'Sofia'. When quoting from their writings, I have retained the version they used of the actress's name. This confusion is also not helped by the fact that Loren plays key roles in two of her major films (*The Gold of Naples* and *Scandal in Sorrento*) as characters with the name of 'Donna Sofia'. Thus the shifting between 'Sophia' and 'Sofia', found throughout the book, is attributable to the variations present in the range of sources consulted on Sophia Loren's career. All translations from Italian are by the author.

Sophia as Nives, the 'Woman of the River'.
Stills Department, Cineteca Nazionale, Rome.

Sophia as Cesira, the antithesis of the pin-up. Stills Department, Cineteca Nazionale, Rome.

1

WHY SOPHIA?

Why Sophia? A study of the career of Sophia Loren has intrinsic interest – she is after all the nearest the nation has to 'an Italian icon' (Gundle 1995: 367) – but it is also important for the insights it affords into the era in which her image was forged. Hers is a career full of contradictions. She came from the poorest and most humble origins, yet came to be associated with glamour and great elegance. In much of her early career she made comedies, yet in her international career few of her films fit that category. Although considered an international star, a retrospective film season of the films of Sophia Loren is virtually unheard of. While the international reputation of postwar Italian cinema is largely based on arthouse productions, Loren's Italian output is wholly defined by the popular genres of comedy and melodrama. Although now seen as highly popular, there were periods of her career when she was vilified, particularly in the Italian press, for her marriage to Carlo Ponti and for the difficulties they later encountered with the Italian tax authorities. And finally, although she is rightly judged to be the one Italian actor of the postwar generation who made a success of her Hollywood career, few of the films that she made in Hollywood had box-office success either in Italy or in the international market. Like any artist, there are two dimensions to her story, the personal and the professional. Loren is generally thought of as a star well known to her public. The bibliography of this book lists numerous biographies of her, as well as books she has authored on beauty, cooking and fashion. From earliest years Loren has fed information about her life to the press, regularly offering individual and syndicated interviews to tell her story. At the same time there has always been huge media coverage of her public image highlighting her many appearances at film festivals in Cannes and Berlin, on-set reports on her films in Hollywood and on location in London, the Oscar successes, and major events in what was supposedly her private life – marriage to the producer Carlo Ponti, and the birth of her two children. It is a type of coverage that has largely neglected to focus on the very considerable importance of her professional career, to the extent that it seems as if she has not merited serious consideration as an artist. This book sets to redress the balance, to fill a major gap in our understanding of Italy's most prominent and enduring star by uncovering and analysing a wealth of information about how she achieved that stardom. It is a book that studies the films of Sophia Loren, but the films are taken also as a means of assessing the context – cultural, historical, industrial – within which her career emerged, the years 1950–64, when the star image of Sophia Loren was moulded.

Sophia Loren is not the only European film artist whose star image has been largely neglected. Indeed, a range of critics have noted the more general absence of a sustained body of analytical work on European stars. Ginette Vincendeau terms star studies in European cinema a 'forgotten category' (1998: 445), while Andy Willis points out that the 'concentration [on Hollywood performers] has overshadowed the operation of stardom within other markets' (2004: 3–4). The hegemony of Hollywood in the film industry itself in turn gives a certain logic to the domination in critical and biographical analysis of Hollywood stars. It also has to be acknowledged that the star system began as one of the major strategies in the marketing of films in early Hollywood (Butler 1998: 345) and as such to a degree remains anchored in the Hollywood system. Italian film-making, particularly in the world market, has built its reputation on arthouse cinema: as a result, in critical terms, much greater importance has been afforded to film directors as the defining presence. One could even argue that critics have given the star treatment to directors of the calibre of Fellini, Visconti and Antonioni rather than to the actors who appeared in their films. In relation to British cinema Bruce Babington argues in a vein similar to Willis and Vincendeau that on 'indigenous stars' there is 'strangely little significant writing' (2001: 3). Babington notes that in *Stars* (1979), the work of Richard Dyer that gave fresh impetus to the field of star studies, Dyer himself addresses, briefly, 'the problematics of applying a theory based on Hollywood stars to other cinemas' (1979: 4). Babington continues:

> [Dyer] writes that he believed that the 'theorising and methodology' underpinning his book are 'broadly applicable' to stars of other cinemas, provided that 'the specificities of these other places where stars are to be found would always have to be respected' (Dyer 1979: 4). In other words, the institutions of film stardom exhibit major constants running across different film cultures, but each national cinema produces different inflections of them. (Babington 2001: 4)

One of the main aims of this book will be to analyse the career of Sophia Loren in relation to the 'inflection' that was the Italian star system of the 1950s, when her career began; and, by clarifying the distinctiveness of that system, to reach an understanding of Loren's career through a focus on the film industry from which her career emerged. In keeping with other European stars, Loren's place in the national film industry – her Italian stardom – derives from a set of structures radically different from those of classical Hollywood. Industrial patterns in the European film market have always been much less stable and much less straightforward to summarize than the Hollywood model. Ginette Vincendeau characterizes European production in general as 'small-scale, fragmented and disorganised' (1998: 442) while Barbara Corsi describes the Italian film industry as 'a random mix of high-minded projects and improvised adventures, developed in the spirit of a game of chance, as if filmmaking was the equivalent of playing roulette' (2001: 10). As a consequence, the study of the career of an individual European star requires close reference to the frequently shifting economic conditions that prevailed at the time of production. As we shall see, in the era following the Second World War the Italian film industry itself evolved with remarkable rapidity and at the same time was modified substantially by changes in the international market following the demise of the Hollywood studio system. Sophia Loren's career was forged in the cinema of 1950s Italy and of Hollywood, and the book will investigate how the structures of national and international cinema shaped her particular brand of stardom.

Questions of national cinemas remain relevant to analysis of the stardom of Sophia Loren, but in the light of recent critical debates the use of the term 'national cinema' requires some clarification. In his initial work on the subject Andrew Higson argued:

> A national cinema is a particular industrial structure; a particular pattern of ownership and control of plant, real estate, human resources and capital, and a system of state legislation which circumscribes the nationality of that ownership – primarily in relation to production. [...] At the level of production, we need to take into account both the means and modes of production employed. (Higson 1989: 42)

Higson has himself revised some of his ideas, particularly the implicit argument of his earlier work that he now believes erroneously assumed that national identity and tradition are already fully formed and fixed in place (2004: 63). In particular, the question of international funding of cinema in the late twentieth century, and the drive to find a cinema with international appeal has blurred the concept of national cinema, and encouraged critics to term film products – from Bond films to the so-called European heritage cinema – as transnational in character. However, broadly speaking it appears that while the validity of the concept of a 'national cinema' continues to be intensely debated and challenged, the notion of a 'national star' is deemed much less problematic. Though few in number, several recent publications on star studies take the notion of the national star as fundamental to their analysis, namely the already cited work on British stars (Bruce Babington 2001), male stars of Spanish cinema (Chris Perriam 2003), and most recently a study of the phases of Italian stardom from the beginnings of cinema to the present (Marcia Landy 2008). At the same time a few monographs on individual stars have been published (very few, if we consider the deluge of material on Hollywood stars and stardom): on Simone Signoret (Susan Hayward 2004), Marcello Mastroianni (Jacqueline Reich 2004) and Catherine Deneuve (Lisa Downing and Sue Harris 2007). Following the route of national stardom does not mean, however, that critics interpret the role of the chosen star purely in relation to national culture. For instance, Downing and Harris view Deneuve as an example of European stars who 'tend to float across a series of national cinemas, bearing the weight of representing their own nationality' (2007: 10–11). Alastair Phillips and Ginette Vincendeau have published a collection of essays (2006) on European stars who tried their fortune in Hollywood but who, as the different analyses show, nevertheless retain in some sense a national labelling be it French (Chevalier) British (Olivier) or German (Dietrich).

This study investigates extensively the particular characteristics of the Italian film industry in the early years of Loren's career in the belief that they offer a valuable route to explicate the ways in which her star identity was constructed. The publications of Gian Piero Brunetta on Italian film history have been an important source of knowledge for this period (2003 and

1998); Thomas Guback (1976 and 1969) and Lorenzo Quaglietti (1980 and 1974) offer two of the few attempts, in English and Italian language respectively, to clarify the funding of the industry, and this area of studies has been very usefully augmented by Chris Wagstaff (1999, 1998, 1995 and 1992) and Barbara Corsi (2002 and 2001). At the same time, Martin Dale's study of Hollywood and the European film industry (1997) gives a very useful, more broad-based overview of the subject. However, with regard to Italian film-making, it is noticeable that these studies do not constitute an extensive or closely integrated body of work. Despite the very necessary commercial dimension – cinema is after all an industry dependent on financial backing and paying customers – there has been greater concentration on the artistic and cultural dimensions, an emphasis true of the present field of film studies in general. This is generally speaking the direction of the innovative work of Stephen Gundle, who has published extensively on the cultural signification of Loren and the other female stars of the period such as Gina Lollobrigida (1999, 1996 and 1995). It is a body of work widely cited, and explicitly acknowledged in Reich's 2004 study of Mastroianni, and Landy's 2008 publication on Italian stardom. Most recently, he has considered the roles of the shapely stars of 1950s Italy as part of a more extensive analysis of the meaning of beauty manifested across the centuries of Italian society (Gundle 2007). At the same time articles of Reka Buckley (2008 and 2006) have shown how the meanings of stardom and female identity in the 1950s may be fruitfully explored through the perspective of fashion and style. However, this means that the subject still remains open to fresh areas of exploration. The intention of this book is to show the value of studying the progress of a star career by linking it to contemporary industrial practices. The career of every artist is inextricably linked to and shaped by the context within which it evolves, a context that in turn largely determines both the prospects and the limitations of that career. As we shall see, the context of Loren's work crosses a number of cultural and industrial models – from early 50s Italy, to late 50s Hollywood, to early 60s Italy and beyond. An analysis of the construction of her star image thus results in greater understanding both of the career of Loren herself and the place of the star – of Europe and of Hollywood – in this most interesting transitional period for film and for postwar culture. The structures this book identifies as subtending the career of Loren, particularly in the context of Italian film-making, are relevant to the careers of many of her contemporaries of greater or lesser stature, from Marcello Mastroianni to Silvana Pampanini, from Marisa Allasio to Alberto Sordi. To this end, the book has relevance beyond the detail of the single star identified in its title.

One of the most recent developments in film studies has been an emphasis on the importance of understanding that, at the level of audience reception, the term 'star' does not signify a single, unified persona but is instead composed of elements that are much more fragmentary in nature. The star image comes about through a process of 'negotiation' (Gledhill 1999: 166) that affords the star a diversity of meanings deriving from the cultural make-up of a range of audience types, all fundamental to the process of producing the star's meaning. Gledhill argues that the experience of reading and viewing is 'a social practice, which differs between groups and historical periods and shapes the meaning audiences derive from cultural products' (Gledhill 1999: 172). A number of critics have based sustained analysis on this premise: Moseley (2003) charts the meanings Audrey Hepburn, a star of the 1950s, might hold for audiences of the late twentieth century. In an earlier study, Jackie Stacey (1994) reviewed the meaning of a range of Hollywood studio stars as perceived by British female audiences. The current study will show that adopting an approach based on diversified meanings of the star image gives particularly rewarding insights into Loren's career: as a product located within separate film cultures, the national-Italian and the international-Hollywood, we shall see that 'Sophia Loren' takes on meanings to be found in the separate, very particular characteristics and audiences of these two main groupings. Throughout the book close reference will be made to Loren's on-screen performance with textual analysis of individual films particularly in the separate case studies; but the films will also be considered more generally as a body of work that raises issues of casting, funding, and the publicity and promotion attendant on the films. In *Stars* Dyer contends that the means by which a star's persona is constructed may be divided under four main headings: promotion, films featuring the star, publicity, and critical reception and comment. Clearly the way that Loren was received and promoted will vary from the equivalent experience of a Hollywood star, but while registering differences in the specific form they take I will demonstrate that these categories remain central to the way Loren's star status is realized. The book concentrates on the years that are crucial to the constructing of the star Sophia Loren: from 1950, when she had her first walk-on film part in Mervyn Le Roy's production *Quo Vadis*, to 1964, when she completes *Marriage Italian Style/Matrimonio all'italiana* directed by Vittorio de Sica. This film was the second of two comedies she made with Marcello Mastroianni on her return to Italian film-making. It follows *Two Women/La ciociara* (1960), where she also worked with De Sica as director, the film that was to mark the climax of her national and international success. The chronology of Loren's career offers natural divisions to map out her ascendancy as a star, and these may be summarized as follows:

Phase 1: beginnings as an Italian national star 1950–7
Phase 2: Hollywood career 1957–60
Phase 3: merging of national and international status 1960–4
Phase 4: transnational star and celebrity 1964–the present

The book's approach, although to some extent chronological, will be subdivided under the headings: Chapter 1: Why Sophia?; Chapter 2: Loren and Ponti; Chapter 3: Loren and Hollywood; Chapter 4: Loren and De Sica; Chapter 5: Loren and Mastroianni; Conclusion: *Cercando (Still Looking For) Sophia*. Chapter 1 is introductory and Chapter 3 considers the Hollywood years. The remaining chapters give focus to Loren's work through the spectrum of three major personalities with whom her star status in closely linked: Carlo Ponti, Vittorio De Sica and Marcello Mastroianni. Each of these chapters includes a case study that offers close analysis of an individual film that at the same time amplifies the main thrust of the chapter's arguments. There are a number of reasons why this division of material offers the more fruitful approach. Firstly, it facilitates a study of the industry through a specific set of professional partnerships: the interaction of Loren with a producer, with a director and with another actor. Thus it becomes a means whereby we understand better both the detail of a single star's career, and the more general industrial framework of the era. Secondly it is proper to argue that a star image does not evolve in purely linear fashion, but is made up of a series of intermittent, non-consecutive phases that combine to produce a whole: Loren's films with Mastroianni cover two distinct chronological phases, but from an artistic perspective can be analysed as a homogenous body of work, where aspects of their separate careers continue to inform the discourse of their on-screen partnership. In the case of De Sica, the partnership is also intermittent, but as will be demonstrated, is productively studied as a unified body of work. Thirdly, such a division of material allows the possibility of addressing the way Loren's star status has been represented both in the critical and the popular press. The attitude is encapsulated in this extract from a *Life* article on her background: 'During those early years Sophia eked out a bare existence [...] then Carlo Ponti came on the scene, her name was changed to Loren, and the famine was over' (Hamblin 1961: 38). Such a perspective is not at all restricted to accounts in the popular international press. Loren is explicitly and repeatedly cited as being guided by a Pygmalion figure – a dominant sophisticated male to her supposedly pliable female role. While biographers Moscati (2005: 97), and Masi and Lancia (2004: 129) assign the Pygmalion role to Carlo Ponti, the film critic Spinazzola (1985: 50) and the film historian Brunetta (1998: 260) characterize De Sica in the same way. There is no doubt that these figures were highly important to Loren's career. In her recent study of the career of Rita Hayworth, Adrienne McLean (2004) shows ways in which, like Loren, Hayworth's public and private life was extensively reported and analysed with particular reference to her marriages and 'the men in her life'. By giving attention to the considerable resources that fed her extra-textual image, we will identify how the press used Loren and how Loren used the press to enhance her career. Like McLean, this book contends that the career of an important star merits fresh consideration. It will provide a clearer and more informed understanding of the role of the individuals and the processes that moulded Sophia.

2

LOREN AND PONTI

Sofia Scicolone was born in Rome on 20 September 1934, but she grew up in the family home of her mother Romilda Villani in Pozzuoli, near Naples. As an aspiring actress she arrived in Rome with her mother in 1950. At this time she was known by the name of her father, Riccardo Scicolone. Her parents had a second child Maria, born in 1937, but they never married. To be illegitimate in the Catholic Italy of this era was exceptionally difficult for any child, and it is not surprising that the various available biographies show that the relationship between the actress and her father remained problematic throughout the duration of their very separate lives.[1] When she began her career Sofia Scicolone made an immediate name change, listing herself in her first professional roles in photo-romance magazines and film-making as Sofia Lazzaro, but she changed the name again, this time to Sophia Loren, when she was cast in *Africa Below the Seas/Africa sotto i mari* (Roccardi, 1952). Accounts of her professional beginnings have suggested that from the moment when she met Carlo Ponti at a Rome nightclub in 1950 the shape of her career – and his role in shaping it – was set, but as Gundle rightly insists, it is clear from all the available evidence that this was not the case (Gundle 1995: 362). Progress was, on the contrary, very gradual. She began in walk-on, non-speaking roles in *Quo vadis* (LeRoy, 1951) and *Anna* (Lattuada, 1952) and bit parts followed in *A Day in Court/Un giorno in pretura* (Steno, 1953), and *The Country of the Campanelli/Il paese dei campanelli* (Boyer, 1954). She moved to more substantial parts in ensemble films to include *The Gold of Naples/L'oro di Napoli* (De Sica, 1954) and *The Sign of Venus/Il segno di Venere* (Risi, 1955), and completed this first phase of her career, the national-Italian phase, playing co-star with Marcello Mastroianni in *Too Bad She's Bad/Peccato che sia una canaglia* (Blasetti, 1954) and *Lucky to be a Woman/La fortuna di essere donna* (Blasetti, 1956). Accounts of Loren's stardom have tended to concentrate on the detail of her specific personal and professional experiences. This chapter adopts a very different focus: it locates Loren as actress and then as star within the general trends of the Italian film industry, with particular emphasis on the distinctive aspects of that industry that shaped her career. It is an approach designed to give greater clarity to the respective roles of the producer Carlo Ponti and the actress Sophia Loren, an approach that contextualizes with greater accuracy the evolution of her nascent star career.

Finding the star

The Italian film industry regrouped quickly after the war, and the drive for postwar reconstruction, manifested initially in the flowering of the neorealist films of Roberto Rossellini, Vittorio De Sica and Luchino Visconti, generated a 'demand for new faces in cinema, theatre and television, that was motivated by democracy and a need for emblematic figures who stood in a general sense for Italy' (Gundle 1999: 378). The quest to discover a new star, particularly a young, shapely female, termed collectively the 'shapely stars' (maggiorate fisiche), was a central focus that gave a very particular complexion to the activities of those recruiting to the industry at the time.[2] There was widespread concern in the contemporary press that actors were securing screen roles without formal professional training. Leading figures such as Marcello Mastroianni and Vittorio Gassman were initially trained in theatre and then progressed to a career in the cinema in the immediate postwar era. At the same time, other ways of accessing the big screen emerged. Neorealist directors adopted the practice of using untrained individuals in their films, with De Sica's casting of the lead role in Bicycle Thieves/Ladri di Biciclette (1948) being the most frequently cited example. But what chiefly concerned film critics was the phenomenon of producers recruiting untrained actresses at the beauty contests that re-emerged soon after the end of the war. Sample headlines give a clear picture of how these developments in casting were viewed in certain circles. The editorial in Cinema nuovo of March 1 1953 was headed 'The Scandal of the Curvaceous Stars' (Lo scandalo delle curve) where the 'scandal' consisted of the fact that, according to the journal, certain actresses were cast in films purely for their looks, and not at all for the quality of their acting skills. In the very next edition there was a follow-up article with the title, '[Actresses] who make films just looking at themselves in the mirror' (Fanno cinema guardandosi allo specchio) (Gandin 1953: 180). The contributor suggested that production companies might take responsibility for funding film schools as a training route for the profession. Producers Domenico Forges Davanzati, Carlo Ponti and Dino De Laurentiis were given the opportunity to respond in future editions: they deemed the strategy to be a good idea but, in practical terms, completely unrealistic (Agnolotti 1953: 332). Later in the same year, and in similar vein, the journal Cinema ran an editorial, 'What are they being given awards for?' (Che cosa si premia?) in which it alleged that in recent films the voices of a number of shapely stars had been dubbed, and that therefore any prizes given them were completely unmerited. Gina Lollobrigida, Silvana Mangano, Eleonora Rossi-Drago, and Silvana Pampanini are identified by name and described as screen personalities who 'don't know how to act, and will never be able to do so' (non sanno, e non saranno mai capaci di recitare) (Callari 1953: 3).[3]

This hostility was to remain a constant factor in estimations of the careers of the shapely stars and their future achievements. Despite this, the industry itself proceeded in improvised fashion to bring new faces to the screen in order to feed the growing popularity of cinema in postwar Italy. Gundle (1996: 37) shows that the beauty contest was a feature of the late Fascist period that took the form of photographic competitions in various magazines. It was revived in 1946, and named Miss Italia. At this point the now-standard parade in evening dress was inaugurated and in 1947 a swimsuit parade was added to the competition format. Though these competitions were not, strictly speaking, casting routes for the film industry, the names of jury members for the 1946 competition reads like a list of talent scouts: two directors, Vittorio De Sica and Luchino Visconti, the actress Isa Miranda, and several scriptwriters – Cesare Zavattini, Giuseppe Marotta, Arrigo Benedetti and Bernardino Palazzi (Faldini and Fofi 1979: 150). The following year, 1947, has been termed 'the golden year of Miss Italia' in that it featured Lucia Bosè, Gina Lollobrigida, Gianna Maria Canale, Silvana Mangano and Eleonora Rossi Drago who all, with varying degrees of success, went on to feature prominently in Italian cinema of the 1950s. In contrast Loren's beginnings in the beauty contests were not at all auspicious.

With the fall of Fascism and the end of the war the relationship of government to Italian film culture also underwent considerable transformation. In June 1947 Giulio Andreotti was appointed as under-secretary in the Department of Entertainment and Tourism; the appointment was re-confirmed after the elections of April 1948, the first held under the new Italian constitution, that saw the Christian Democrats take power with a substantial majority. He held the post until 1953, one of the longest appointees to the position. Fascism had operated the national film industry as a subsidised industry and formalized its funding structures in the Alfieri law of 1938, and a similar system of state control and funding was revived in this initial period of postwar Italian democracy. As with other government administrators in the subsidised film industries of postwar Europe, Andreotti's role required him to balance the demands of national cinema with the pressures exerted by Hollywood, which at first flooded Europe with American-made films that could not be screened during the war years. However, by the early 1950s the American film industry had other reasons for looking to Europe as a market. The US landmark Paramount ruling of 1949 imposed a separation of production and distribution practices, bringing to an end the structure of vertical integration that was fundamental to the Hollywood studio system. As the industry adjusted to this radical change in its way of functioning, the studios began to target Europe both as a location and market for film-making.[4] The 1950s were marked by the era of the so-called 'runaway productions' (films funded by American money, using European locations and technical personnel). Mervyn LeRoy's Quo Vadis made at Rome's Cinecittà in 1950 was the first film of this type, where Loren had her first walk-on part. Under the direct auspices of Andreotti, the national industry capitalized on the American presence in Italy through a series of measures incorporated into two separate laws of 1949, the first passed in July, termed the little law (leggina) and major law (grande) of December that came to be known as 'the Andreotti law'.

The first of these pieces of legislation required all importers of foreign films to pay a levy to have them dubbed into Italian. Monies raised in this way, further augmented by direct government contributions, then became the source of loans granted at favourable rates to finance national film-making projects that 'amounted to taxing American films and lending the money to Italian producers' (Wagstaff 1995: 100). With the source of funding established, the second law set out procedures required of Italian producers to qualify for these monies. Producers submitted documentation to a 'technical committee' that had the power to veto or approve not only the project itself, but also monies for the project.[5] Even if a producer managed to raise sufficient funds to make a film independently, it would still be impossible to screen the film in the public domain without required government approval (the so-called nulla osta).

Detailed studies of the consequences of this legislation are agreed that it established a level of governmental control tantamount to censorship, demonstrated not least in the way it successfully blunted the approach, central to neorealism, of presenting a critique of contemporary society (Corsi 2001: 58–9; Forgacs 1989: 61; Wagstaff 1995: 101). In their account of the film industry of the 1950s, Bizzarri and Solaroli argue that this contradicted the provisions of the new constitution regarding free speech, and in fact imposed on the film industry a policy more in keeping with the restrictions of Fascist public order policies of the 1920s (Bizzarri and Solaroli 1958: 44). Without doubt Andreotti and the laws of 1949 set the direction of postwar Italian film-making but to a degree; just as became apparent in debates about training screen actors, cultural debates were swept aside by the impetus of those working in the industry itself who, in the face of the various government pressures, channelled their creative energies into other cinematic styles.[6] There followed a series of highly successful comedy films, a form of popular cinema fundamental to Loren's early career, that triggered a new era of box-office hits (Corsi 2001: 59). The popularity of these comic films was such that it has been suggested that it is in their freshness and vigour, rather than in neorealism, that the climate of postwar Italy is more truly reflected (Ellwood 1999: 825). Coinciding with this decisive period for the political and cultural complexion of postwar Italy came Giuseppe De Santis' *Bitter Rice/Riso amaro* (1949), the film that set a direction central to the star-making strategies of Loren's (and not only Loren's) career. Producers recognized that the diva image of Silvana Mangano in the lead role contributed substantially to the film's great national and international success and as a result they looked to continue down the route opened up by this film (Brunetta 1998: 256). *Bitter Rice* fits without doubt the category of box-office hit. It was the first major success for a participant in the beauty contests of the late 1940s; it inaugurated the era of the 'shapely stars', the group of screen actresses of which Loren soon became a part; and it established them as the major figures, one could argue the sole figures, of a short-lived star system of Italian character. This was the scenario that presented itself to the producer Ponti and the actress Loren as the industry moved into the 1950s.

The producer and the studio: Ponti before Loren

By the time Ponti and Loren met in 1950 Ponti had already been working very successfully in the Italian film industry for ten years. So while 1950 marked the beginnings of Loren's career and a changing agenda for the national film industry, it was also the start of a fresh chapter in the history of Ponti's career as a producer, when he set up an independent production company with Dino De Laurentiis, another producer who first worked with him at the Lux studio. Ponti was born in Magenta, near Milan in 1912, and like his father, he qualified as a lawyer. He came to film-making through one of his father's clients Antonio Mambretti, a Milanese businessman involved in the publishing business. In 1938 Mambretti, in conjunction with a number of other business colleagues, set up the film production company, Artisti Tecnici Associati (ATA). Ponti has said he was initially engaged as lawyer to Mambretti's new enterprise, but quickly became involved instead in the film-making side of the business (Della Casa 2003: 81). As a result in 1940 he produced his and the company's first film, *Old Fashioned World/Piccolo mondo antico* shot mainly in the FERT film studios in Turin. The film was a considerable success, and is generally credited with enhancing the star status of the young Alida Valli. Filming continued in Italy during the war years until September 1943 when, following the fall of Mussolini, the country came under German occupation and film production was suspended. In September 1943 Ponti was working for ATA on location near Rome on a film directed by Alberto Lattuada, *The Arrow/Una freccia nel fianco*. When Rome was liberated in June 1944 production slowly began again. The Lux film company bought the rights to Lattuada's film, and with Ponti as its producer *The Arrow* was completed as an ATA-Lux co-production in 1945, one of the first films to be released in Italy after the end of the war.

Thereafter, Ponti worked consistently with Lux Film until 1950, when he embarked on a series of more independent ventures. The following career summary shows the total production figures for each film company with which Ponti was involved. With the exception of Lux, where he was obviously only part of a much bigger enterprise, the figures give a good indication of the number of films for which over the years, Ponti's production companies had sole or joint (with De Laurentiis) responsibility:

1940–45	company director and producer for ATA (7 films)
1945–50	producer for Lux Film (141 films)
1950–55	company director and producer for Ponti-De Laurentiis spa (32 films)
1950–65	company director and producer for Carlo Ponti Cinematografica spa (9 films)
1952–55	Rosa Film spa (8 films)
1956–62	company director and producer for Carlo Ponti spa (9 films)
1959–77	company director and producer for Compagnia Cinematografica Champion spa (73 films)

Source: Bernardini (2000), *Cinema italiano 1930–1995: le imprese di produzione*, Rome: ANICA.

Bernardini does not list Ponti in the company credits of Rosa Film but it is widely accepted that Ponti set up this production company with De Laurentiis, seeing it as a golden opportunity to produce the films of the popular Italian comic Totò. The success of the low-budget Totò films enabled him and De Laurentiis to leave Lux and set up their own joint production company (Ruffin 2002: 268)[7], and this is confirmed by Ponti himself in a retrospective summary of his career (Della Casa 2003: 161). Interestingly, various Totò projects had been offered to Lux, but the studio consistently refused to 'do comedy', a policy that ultimately proved extremely harmful to its long-term financial prospects (Farassino and Sanguineti 1984: 71).

To appreciate the place of the producer and the actor in the industry we must explore further the ways in which production companies of the era functioned. Terms such as 'star' and 'studio' relate to the structures of the standardised Hollywood industry. The terms carry a different meaning when applied to the European film industry, and this requires clarification. In Italian cinema there was no standardized mode of production, but rather a kind of ad-hoc tradition that emerged from the efforts of individual production companies. The two main companies that predominated in the years of Loren's early career were Lux and Titanus.[8] The history of these studios is shown in the following summary:

	LUX	TITANUS
year of founding	1934	1904
location of founding	Turin	Naples
year of transfer to Rome	1940	1928
head of studio in 1950s	Riccardo Gualino	Goffredo Lombardo

Lux and Titanus operated very different modes of production. Lux was 'a studio without studios'(Farassino and Sanguineti 1984: 182). Its headquarters were a set of offices, with no facilities or designated space for shooting, which had to be hired separately. Once a project was agreed with Lux, the company guaranteed the means of distribution and exhibition. This was of considerable advantage to those targeting the international market because, exceptionally, Lux set up a strong export system with agencies in a range of locations in Europe, South America, the Middle East and the United States (Wagstaff 1998: 76). Titanus was closer to the vertically integrated model of the Hollywood studio, providing the means of production (studios and equipment for shooting, editing and dubbing facilities) as well as the means of distribution and exhibition: however, its distribution network was much smaller than that of Lux. Heads of studio Riccardo Gualino and Goffredo Lombardo are classified simply as producers, but in fact they provided private finances to fund the studios so that they performed a dual role of both financier and producer of the films that carried the name of their production companies. In their different ways they are viewed as visionary individuals carrying out a studio policy (politica) that shaped the film industry both commercially and culturally.[9]

Beyond Gualino and Lombardo there existed a separate tier of individuals, also termed producers, but who played a rather different role in the film-making process. This group included Ponti, De Laurentiis and others such as Antonio Mambretti, David Forges Davanzati and Luigi Rovere who all for a time worked at Lux. Irrespective of the mode of production, all Italian production companies of the period had the same working relationship with this tier of producers whom they hired to work on a film-by-film basis. The industry lacked the long-term stability necessary to offer employees a long-term, binding contract. The rapid rise and fall of the various production companies in this period meant that, even for those few employees who held long-term contracts, such arrangements were short-lived.[10] In this respect the role of the Italian film producer (for the present we will consider this one role) resembles closely that of the producer not of the Hollywood studio system, but of the system that followed its dismantling. Janet Staiger dates from 1955 the inception of what she labels 'the package-unit system' under which 'the producer organised a film project; he or she secured financing and combined the necessary laborers and the means of production (the narrative property, the equipment and the physical sites of production)' (Staiger 1985: 330). This was precisely the agenda for Italian producers of the type of Ponti, active in the postwar period. They secured approval and funding for a proposed film project from two separate sources: firstly private funds from the studio and secondly, following the terms established in the Andreotti Law, public funds that were issued in a combination of grants and loans.[11] Ponti and his fellow producers were to a large extent 'schooled' at the Lux studio (Brunetta 1998: 238). The mode of production at Lux ensured that what they learned were the skills necessary to package the unit, negotiating all the processes, artistic and financial, that this required, and delivering the end product, potentially a commercially successful film. These were the skills that Ponti brought to the next phase of his career, when he worked with Sophia Loren.

This account raises interesting questions about critical approaches to European cinema. One of the standard perspectives on arthouse cinema has been the auteur-led approach that identifies the director as the defining sensibility of the film. Such an approach has been consistently challenged since the auteur theory was first mooted by the *Cahiers du cinema* group in the 1950s. However our observation of the studios of Lux and Titanus raises the possibility of a variation to that approach. In his summary of the achievements of the Titanus studio Barlozetti states that 'Everyone remembers Goffredo Lombardo as a *produttore-autore* (producer-auteur), the ambitious protagonist of an unrepeatable era of Italian filmmaking', and goes so far as to describe Lombardo as *produttore-divo* – both producer and star of the show (2000: 25). The director Dino Risi also uses the term producer-auteur to describe the role of Franco Cristaldi at the production company Vides (Barlozetti 1980: 41). At Vides, Cristaldi was responsible for producing important films of the 1960s that included Francesco Rosi's *Salvatore Giuliano* (1961). Contemporary analysis of the subject is found in an article entitled, 'The producer is (also) the creator of the film', by Renato Gualino, son of Riccardo Gualino, the head of Lux, in which he argues for the producer to be recognized as a 'unique, co-ordinating force in realizing a film' (Gualino 1950: 156). Of course the question implicit in the title of Gualino's essay, 'Who is the creator of a film?' is not in itself valid: as with debates on the role of the director as auteur, a film's authorship cannot be assigned to an individual as the single creative source. These arguments are however an interesting source from within the contemporary industry that serve to highlight the importance of the role that the producer, be it Gualino, Lombardo or Ponti, played in the film-making of this era. We will now consider the implications of these structures for the career of Loren.

The actress and the producer: Loren and Ponti
Most accounts of the Loren-Ponti relationship assert that there existed a legally binding contract cementing their professional relationship (Rondi 1998: 298; Masi and Lancia 2004: 231). Even a recent obituary of Carlo Ponti includes the statement that Loren was placed under contract to him from an early point in her career (D'Agostini 2007: 48). This understanding is completely contradicted by the files of the Italian Central State Archive in Rome which instead show that throughout her time in the Italian cinema of the 1950s, Loren worked on a film-by-film basis. The myth of a Loren-Ponti contract is even more puzzling when we realize that the Ponti–De Laurentiis production company was one of the very few to offer actors more long-term arrangements (See Appendix B: Archive Sample 1). Contracts issued in the early 1950s by Ponti–De Laurentiis did not run their full course, however, since the company itself was dissolved in 1955. Our summary of the workings of Lux and Titanus shows that no standard model existed for an Italian film studio, nor for the conditions of employment of those who worked for the studio. This information has implications central to an understanding of the place of the actor in what is termed 'the market of performance labour' (McDonald 1998: 196), here precisely

the labour market in which Sophia Loren and other Italian stars of the period operated. It is fundamental to emphasize that the labour of all personnel in Italian film-making, artistic (including actor, director, producer, scriptwriter) and technical (including cameraman, costume designer, set designer, lighting operator), operated on a freelance basis. Pay levels and conditions of employment for technical staff were fixed by the various trade union agreements in operation. Beyond this, for major players in the film-making process – directors, leading cameramen, valued scriptwriters – levels of payment were negotiable, but terms offered by the employing production company remained governed by a markedly unstable industrial context. Even a director like Dino Risi, responsible for some of the great films of the Italian comedy tradition, testified to his experience at Titanus, saying that 'we didn't have contracts; if we were lucky they sometimes offered us options on a second film' (Barlozetti 1980: 41).

In the preceding chapter it was emphasized that the structures of the Italian film industry vis-à-vis the star were radically different from the Hollywood model. Stardom evolved from within the earliest structuring of Hollywood and became a central feature of the studio system. In our survey of Lux and Titanus it emerges that the production practices of these studios closely resembled what Staiger terms the Hollywood 'package unit' system that replaced the system of the self-contained studio. It follows from this that, just as in the case of the producer, the status of the Italian actor/star may in fact be validly paralleled with that of a Hollywood employee – not a studio-era star, but rather a star of the post-studio era. Without doubt substantial differences in the funding of the separate industries remained. As we have seen, Italian cinema was funded by a combination of state subsidy and private enterprise; on the other hand Hollywood's financial backing derives solely from the private sector. This may well have an impact on the star's potential earnings: for example, a film-by-film contract in Hollywood, with its larger market and funding sources, might include the guarantee of the star's share of a film's profits. In 1950s Italy contracts for leading players show that, with few exceptions, payment was made by a pre-established set fee. Questions of the sources of funding are however secondary to this analysis: the prime focus is the status of the star within a given funding system, and the implications of that status for the career of an individual star. MacDonald (2005: 196) argues that, following the decline of the Hollywood studio system, freelance labour had the effect of making actors highly dependent on agents, casting officers and unions to mediate between performer and industry, and Staiger reinforces the point stating that workers' employment was based 'on a film, not a firm' (Staiger 1985: 330). Italian screen actors never worked in a 'firm' like the Hollywood majors, with the practices that governed the work of the studio stars of the 30s and 40s. Terms such as 'informal' (Barlozetti 1980: 41) and 'artisan' (Guback 1976: 398) have been used to reflect the character of the industry of the 1950s. This helps us to understand the conditions that governed the professional relationship between any Italian producer and Italian star. As Loren's filmography shows, the situation was indeed informal, and the prevailing custom was that the actor moved from one film, from one package-unit to another, without any binding contract, without any clear definition to the trajectory of his/her career. Ironically, in the Hollywood-studio era professional independence was a much sought-after goal, and there are a number of famous cases of challenges to studio power made by stars such as Olivia De Havilland and Bette Davis, dissatisfied with the binding nature of their contracts. Staiger however shows that others were happy to hone their skills under the secure employment conditions that the studio gave them, although it is worth noting that the opinions she cites as favourable to the studio system belong to those who worked behind rather than in front of the camera – art director George Gibson and cinematographer Hal Rossen who both worked at MGM (Staiger 1985: 337).

Notionally, then, both Hollywood and Italian stars of Loren's time found themselves in the same contractual position. However, substantial differences remained, the major one being that in Italy there were very few formal routes in place to negotiate for and protect the interests of the star. Evidence of concerted industrial organization and the creation of a trade union dates from slightly later, from 1960 to be exact, the year in which actors Gino Cervi, Marcello Mastroianni, Nino Manfredi and Enrico Maria Salerno formed the Italian Actors Union (Società Attori Italiani) that embraced members working in cinema, theatre and television (Cavalli: 2007).[12] Both Lux and Titanus had press offices, but naturally these offices concentrated on representing the interests of the studio, rather than those of the individual employee/star. In Hollywood the post-studio era was marked by the rise of powerful agencies such as the MCA of Lew Wasserman. The profits-only deal that Wasserman brokered with Universal Studios for James Stewart's lead role in Winchester '73 (Anthony Mann, 1950) is generally seen as symptomatic of a changed agenda for Hollywood and its stars. It is taken as marking the rise of the agent as well as the increased power of the individual freelance star (Gomery 2005: 195). In Italy press agents such as Lucherini and Spinola came to the fore in the late 1950s, and were significant to Loren's later career, when she returned to the ambit of Italian film-making in the early 1960s. Accounts of their improvised methods of publicising the stars contrast sharply with Wasserman's hard-headed, assertive style (Lucherini and Spinola 1984). But drawing this comparison has limited value: what must be emphasized is rather the differences in the structures within which the so-called 'agents' operated. Dale gives crucial clarification of the point when he argues that, 'Europe does not have agents along the Hollywood model, because the principal "clients" in the business are not commercial entities, but the state' (Dale 1997: 229). The function of the 'agent' in the European film industry was thus restricted simply to the level of carrying out press or publicity activities for the given star. An 'agent' in Hollywood played a very different role: a practitioner such as Wasserman was engaged instead in negotiating the most lucrative possible contract of employment between his client and the private company funding the film. In Italy, as we have seen, funding was drawn from a combination of monies from the state, and from companies like Titanus and Lux. Within this framework, what powers of negotiation existed for remunerating the star, clearly much less significant than in the Hollywood equivalent, would thus be mainly within the remit of the producer who set up the production package.

This scenario surely goes far in explaining why so many relationships combining the personal and the professional flourished in the postwar era of Italian film-making between (male) producer and (female) star. Despite variations in their respective roles, such a list would certainly include: Carlo Ponti and Sophia Loren; Dino De Laurentiis and Silvana Mangano; Alfredo Guarini and Isa Miranda; Franco Cristaldi and Claudia Cardinale. Inasmuch as the director's status may have facilitated funding, a similar career pattern may be noted involving (male) director and (female) star. This in no way suggests comment on the career potential and skills of the individual actress, simply on the financial realities of the industry in the period. Such a list would include: Michelangelo Antonioni and Monica Vitti; Federico Fellini and Giulietta Masina; Alberto Lattuada and Carla del Poggio; Riccardo Freda and Gianna Maria Canale; Renato Castellani and Maria Fiore; scriptwriter Sergio Amidei and actress Giovanna Ralli. Beyond the confines of Italian cinema, we might look also at parallels with the role of Roger Vadim in relation to Brigitte Bardot (the same age as Loren, but whose first major film was in 1956) and Annette Stroyberg, as well as his efforts to shape the careers of Catherine Denueve and Jane Fonda. Ponti himself makes characteristically robust comment on his methods of managing the career of potential stars (it is interesting to note that before working with Loren, he was also briefly linked to the career of Gina Lollobrigida):

> Sophia and Lollobrigida began their careers miming the main parts in opera films. This was a career start that had, as I saw it, no real future, and we dropped it almost as soon as it began: singers never succeed as actresses. I have to say that actresses who have control over their career just don't exist. It is possible that talented male stars might manage to establish an independent career for themselves. But in the whole history of cinema there is not one actress, and I mean not a single one, from Garbo to Dietrich, whose career has taken off without the help of a man. (Farassino 2000: 13)

Ponti's comments demonstrate no doubt the level of paternalism present in the mentality of the contemporary industry, but at the same time it is pointless to view the workings of Italian cinema (and not only Italian cinema) of the 1950s from a present-day perspective. Even today a star such as Jodie Foster, who has created for herself a wealth of career options as actress, director and producer remains exceptional, and such prospects would certainly have been impossible in Loren's time. Nevertheless, by giving close attention to the industrial structures that were in place, it is surely possible to give an account of the role of the star of the 1950s that is more informed and more sharply focused. It has been common practice to present the relationships listed, especially those relating to popular cinema and the fortunes of Loren's star grouping, the shapely stars, as some kind of romantic formula whereby a struggling young actress was taken on, granted screen roles and married by a benevolent producer/director. Such accounts personalize the issue to the point where neither party is viewed as part of a professional, industrialized system the workings of which impact directly on their roles. One of the main aims of this analysis is to establish a more valid basis for delineating the Loren–Ponti relationship, to show that it is driven not solely by the narrative of their personal, individual histories. It proposes instead that this and similar relationships developed as a direct consequence of the modes of production that predominated at the time. Loren and Ponti may thus be accurately viewed as representative, if exceptional, figures in a determinate industrial and commercial framework. With this framework in mind, we will now consider the detail of the Italian career that first moulded Sophia.

Early career: The photo-romances

Despite what appeared to be a promising start, the securing of a walk-on part in Quo vadis shortly after her arrival in Rome, Sophia Loren's progress to stardom was anything but rapid. She had limited success in the round of beauty contests because her looks did not fit the expectation of the time for what constituted a typical Italian beauty. Debates around these contests threw up interesting questions of the relationship between the physicality of the 'shapely stars' and what were considered the more traditional forms of Italian beauty: Loren, it is suggested, was 'too dark and earthy, her mouth was too large and she was too tall', and, most significantly 'her blossoming figure suggested more torbid passions than was deemed appropriate for the average beauty queen' (Gundle 1995: 370). She had some success, but overall results were modest: 1949 runner-up in the 'Queen of the Sea' competition in Naples; consolatory title of 'Miss Elegance' in the 1950 Miss Italia competition; and second place at Rome's Colle Oppio nightclub, where Ponti first met her, and invited her to take part in the beauty contest that was in progress. Following this first meeting Ponti arranged a screen test, but no offers of roles were forthcoming (Faldini and Fofi 1979: 221). She continued to play a number of minor screen parts, but in the period 1950 to 1952 her main employment was in the popular photo-romance magazines of the period and, to a lesser extent, in the cine-romance magazines (which will be discussed in the chapter case study). Taking the name of Sofia Lazzaro, she played the lead role in three photo-romance narratives published in *Sogno* and two in *Cine Illustrato*. She debuted in the romance 'Forbidden Love' (*Non posso amarti*) in *Sogno* on 19 November 1950, figuring on the front cover in the issue of 2 December 1950. Her final role was the lead in 'The Beautiful Intruder' (*L'adorabile intrusa*) and this stage of her career was marked by a farewell cover of *Sogno* in April 1953.

Sogno was one of three major photo-romance magazines that began publication in the postwar period. The first of these publications was *Grand Hotel* issued by the Milan publishers Universo on 29 June 1946, and the magazine was so successful that it triggered similar publications in the following year of *Sogno* (published by Rizzoli) and *Bolero Film* (published by Mondadori).[13] The photo-romances consisted of narratives of forbidden passions in the style of classic melodrama. In general, each weekly edition contained two or three separate stories alongside topical showbiz material, and adverts for beauty and household products. In the picture romances Loren was generally assigned the role of seductress, such as in *Cine Illustrato*'s 'The Garden of Allah' (*Il giardino di Allah*) where she plays Irene, a dark-eyed belly dancer whose role and appearance contrast sharply with Domina, a fair-haired safari-suited tourist, played by one Ingrid Swenson. To a degree this role conforms to an aspect individual to Loren, the excess suggested in her non-conforming physicality. However, the practice is evident from the very first issue of *Grand Hotel*, dated 29 June 1946, where illustrations for the story 'The Tears of Gold' (*Le lacrime d'oro*) show a 'western' protagonist in safari dress set against scantily-clad 'oriental' women of the maharajah's harem (Bravo 2003: 97). This representation of the extremes of female identity was common in the melodrama, a media form articulating aspects of female sexuality in a period of very marked social change. What part did the photo-romances play in developing Loren's image? Loren herself has spoken dismissively of her work at this time calling it 'the most stupid job imaginable' (Faldini and Fofi 1979: 152). This perspective, not uncommon for those who went on to a successful cinema career, underestimates the importance of the medium, as well as undervaluing it as a means to establish the potential of a star in the public consciousness. Instead the photo-romance may be seen as an important stage in developing Loren's image. It fed a very real demand for the narratives of melodrama, a highly popular subject-matter that the cinema of the time only partially fulfilled (De Berti 2002: 116). As a visual medium it also provided an opportunity to develop and refine Loren's image in relation to the camera, in this case the still camera. While *Grand Hotel* consistently used sketched drawings until the mid-1950s, from their inception *Sogno* and *Bolero* worked with photographic images. The published visuals of the narratives were thus the result of what might be termed an extended photo-shoot. Loren/Lazzaro's first cover for *Sogno* in 1950 presents her as a gauche, unsophisticated young girl. If we compare this cover to her final role as Tatiana in *The Beautiful Outsider* where she wears a low-cut strapless dress, hair and makeup carefully married to an altogether more polished style, the process of grooming is evident. The photo-romance certainly offered to the public a sustained means of accessing her image. Along with the cine-romances, begun in 1952, the magazines were available to buy from the news-stand, but could also be purchased by subscription, posted out weekly or monthly depending on frequency of publication. They could thus additionally reach those who lived in provincial locations, perhaps without access to a cinema.

In the period of Loren's photo-romance work her film roles were very much bit parts, roles in ensemble pieces such as Elvira, one of the potential victims of traffickers in *The White Slave Trade*; or as Sisina, lead in one of the musical sketches of *Neapolitan Carousel/Carosello napoletano* (Giannini, 1953). At this stage it was not at all clear which medium would predominate in her career. Some of her co-stars of the time such as Corrado Alba never progressed beyond the photo-romance; Mauro Vellani, paired with her in 'The Beautiful Outsider' took the screen name Antonio Cifariello and played roles in a number of successful films such as Nicolino, Loren's young suitor in *Scandal in Sorrento/Pane amore e...* (Risi, 1954) but at best his career can be described as that of a jobbing actor. The photo-romance did not function in a way directly comparable to the relationship between filmic and non-filmic materials of classic Hollywood. Ellis argues that in the studio era the figure of the performer was first established as star on the cinema screen, and then entered into subsidiary forms of circulation that fed back into future film performances (Ellis 1982: 234). The photo-romance instead played a more variable role in enhancing a given actor's career. For those such as Loren and Gina Lollobrigida it formed the starting point, while leading actors like Vittorio Gassman and Massimo Girotti made guest appearances, taking up central roles in photo-romances later in the decade, when they were already well-established screen personalities (De Berti 2002: 234). The photo-romance thus played a very singular role in postwar Italian culture while at the same time serving the important function of bringing Sofia Lazzaro to the attention of a wide-ranging public.

Early career: The films

In 1953 the Sofia Lazzaro of photo-romances changed her name to Sophia Loren. The main body of her career as Italian star was concentrated over a brief time-span, when she moved rapidly from one film project to another. Her output in this brief period consists largely of the films termed 'pink neorealism' (*neorealismo rosa*) the forerunner of the body of Italian comedy films (*commedia all'italiana*) that lasted into the 1960s and beyond. There is additionally one super-production *Attila* (Francisci, 1954) and one melodrama, *The Woman of the River/La donna del fiume* (Soldati, 1955), focus of the chapter case study. She played roles in five major comedies that may be subdivided in accordance with their setting and more general discourse between the rural/provincial: *The Miller's Beautiful Wife/La bella mugnaia* (Camerini, 1955),

Scandal in Sorrento (1955) and the contemporary urban: *The Sign of Venus/Il segno di Venere* (Risi, 1954), *Too Bad She's Bad* (1954), and *Lucky to Be a Woman* (1956). The first group without doubt builds on the success of her role in *The Gold of Naples*. It continues to align her with her Neapolitan origins, a direction already traceable in the secondary roles she had played in *Neapolitan Carousel* (1954) and *Poverty and Nobility/Miseria e Nobiltà* (Mattoli, 1953). The scripting of these films draws on the very rich tradition of Neapolitan comic theatre in the writings of Eduardo De Filippo, and the short stories of Giuseppe Marotta that were first published in serialized form in *Corriere della Sera* between 1942 and 1947. Loren's work with these writers is revived again in her comedies with Marcello Mastroianni ten years later, and collaborations with De Sica and Mastroianni will be more fully explored in Chapters 4 and 5 respectively.

The Neapolitan material offered a distinguishing dimension to Loren's persona. It marked her as a woman of the people, with her non-traditional physical qualities and provincial identity serving as a means of establishing and differentiating her from other aspiring stars of the period. Two recurrent elements of the star-making process are at work here. On the one hand there is the tendency to locate a particular personality within a type or grouping, compartmentalizing him/her in a way that facilitates easy assimilation into the popular consciousness (MacDonald 2005: 11). On the other hand from earliest times there is the desire for the star to arrive at 'monopoly status'. This is important for the film-makers, who use the star as a means of product differentiation to maximize their profits, and for the star who, once established as a form of monopoly product, commands correspondingly higher fees for his/her work (Butler 1998: 345). Both aspects have relevance to Loren's career at this time, and are particularly revealed in her casting in the third film of the *Bread and Love* cycle where she replaced Gina Lollobrigida as the co-star of Vittorio De Sica. We may recall that, following the triumph of *Bitter Rice*, producers looked to repeat the success of the film and of Silvana Mangano as its protagonist. In this third film of the series Loren took up a role already familiar to a public not at all sated with their indigenous stars, eager for more faces to feed the impetus of the new Italy. In this sense it is suggested that she drew advantage from being marginally younger than the two main forerunners of the group, Mangano and Lollobrigida.

The pattern of the careers of Loren and Lollobrigida were for a time almost analogous, 'as if Sofia (sic) was following precisely in the footsteps of Gina' (Spinazzola 1985: 128). Lollobrigida, like Loren, had appeared in photo-romances, opera films, and then in the first two films of the series, *Bread, Love and Dreams /Pane amore e fantasia* (Comencini, 1953) and *Bread, Love and Jealousy/ Pane amore e gelosia* (Risi, 1954). But what is more, taking on the role offered the possibility that through association with the stardom of Lollobrigida, Loren might even eventually eclipse the success of her already established rival (Rondi 1998: 300). The cast list on the film's original budget listed Lollobrigida in the female lead role, but later documentation replaced her name with that of Loren (ACS/PF/*Scandal in Sorrento*). The reasons for Lollobrigida's withdrawal from the third film of the series were the subject of much speculation, but the decision had a logic that teamed with her subsequent career choices where, despite possessing a strong talent for comedy, she seemed for a while intent on proving her worth in a series of major dramatic, non-comedy roles (Spinazzola 1985: 127). The decision of Lollobrigida gave Loren the opportunity to sustain her momentum as a recent addition to the successes of the 'shapely stars'. From a different perspective however, this route could be seen as disadvantageous to the long-term commercial durability of a rising star. It was certainly the case, and here Lollobrigida's intuition was not at all mistaken, that within Italian comedy the various mini-cycles such as *Bread and Love* and a subsequent group that began with *Poor but Handsome/Poveri ma belli* (Risi, 1957), had rapid success but with repetition quickly lost the potential to enhance a star career.

The various strands of Loren's Italian career draw to a most interesting conclusion in the reception of the last film of this period, *Lucky to Be a Woman*. The film was premiered in Cortina d'Ampezzo in January 1956 when she was about to start filming her first American production *The Pride and the Passion* in Spain. At this time the ski resort was hosting the Winter Olympics and, being already full of press representatives, was a prime location for promoting the film. Press reports fuelled the supposed rivalry between the two actresses indicating that Gina Lollobrigida was planning a trip to the resort carefully timed to avoid meeting Loren directly. A contemporary report on the event in *Il messaggero* is typical of the standard press handling of a film's premiere (De Monte: 1956). It says little about the film itself, and a great deal about how Loren was dressed, listing which leading media figures and local dignitaries attended the event, the huge crowds gathered to see the stars, and what happened at the post-screening party. Such a success, the paper suggests, was bound to harm the follow-up visit of Lollobrigida. However, perhaps most importantly, the report classifies Loren as 'shapely star number two' (*maggiorata fisica numero due*) in anticipation of the arrival of Lollobrigida, designated to be still the number one star of the group. Although an apparently throwaway line, it is significant in pinpointing the limitations for the potential of Loren's career within the Italian film industry of the period. Even if she succeeded in securing the title of 'shapely star number one', this was still an achievement that suggested distinct restrictions to the trajectory of her career. One can foresee her as remaining a differentiated type within an established category ('the Neapolitan shapely star'), but not necessarily progressing to command the desired position of all stars and those who promote the stars, that of monopoly status. This was a status she achieved only after she left the Italian film industry to pursue her fortunes in Hollywood, a career move considered in the next chapter.

Case study: The Woman of the River/La donna del fiume (Soldati, 1954)

The Woman of the River merits close attention for a number of reasons. By the time Loren made the film her persona was established on screen almost entirely through a rapid series of comic roles thus linking her to the standard narrative pattern of comedy where obstacles to the lovers' romance are resolved in a light-hearted, harmonious conclusion. The part she plays in *The Woman of the River* – that of a young worker in the Po valley beloved and then abandoned by the father of her newly born child – does not marry with these comic associations. The film is a melodrama, with strong traces of the neorealist tradition found in extensive location shooting in the Comacchio area of the Po delta, and the use of non-professional cast, drawn from workers local to the area. At the same time it has regularly been interpreted as devised to give a star role to Loren, as a vehicle intended to further her career potential. This may well be so, but if we accept that postwar Italian cinema was driven by a need for emblematic figures who stood in a general sense for Italy (Gundle 1995: 370), it is important to underline that Loren's role in this film may be seen to 'stand for' a very different kind of Italy from that proposed by her comic roles. On screen she plays a part full of contradictions that mark the struggle to redefine gender identity and gender relations that, off screen, was true of a society adapting to the social changes of the postwar period. *The Woman of the River* is also important because the detail of its production and promotion gives insight into the place of the film, and the place of Carlo Ponti, in this phase of Loren's career.

Producing the film

The Woman of the River was a film conceived during the period of operation of Ponti–De Laurentiis spa, but eventually attributed to Ponti Cinematografica/Excelsa. Ponti and Dino De Laurentiis worked individually and together at Lux until 1950, when they broke away to form their own production company. With their energy and drive they were by then termed 'the young lions' of the industry (Corsi 2002: 38), who aggressively worked the system, securing funding from a range of sources that ranged from European co-production deals to American capital investment and distribution contracts. The main period of their collaboration 1950-6 – the duration of their independent production company – shows a most remarkable run of successes for the partnership, not least in the range of film they produced: from popular national comedies such as *The Gold of Naples* to arthouse productions, *La strada* (Fellini, 1954) and the Italian blockbuster made with Paramount funding, *War and Peace* (King Vidor, 1956). Despite the change of employment from Lux to their own company, we can say that the mode of production remained largely the same in that they themselves continued to operate a film-by-film package-unit system. Production arrangements for Loren's films in this period demonstrate that to term them an 'independent production company' is somewhat misleading. In fact few films of her films were registered as funded wholly by Ponti–De Laurentiis. For example, they packaged *Attila* with Lux funding, while Paramount, which had secured distribution rights for *The Gold of Naples* before filming began, contributed substantially to that film's initial budget. Commentators offer mixed opinions on this mode of operation. Sanguineti argues that:

> it was a stroke of genius on Ponti's part that he never really severed links with the Lux film company. On the contrary, part of him never left. We could say he kept one foot in the door of Lux, and the other two feet outside. (Farassino and Sanguineti 1984: 85)

The director Giuseppe De Santis viewed the strategy even less sympathetically, describing Ponti and his partner as 'examples of contractors who made films with other people's money' (Barlozetti 1980: 150). However, whatever the funding sources – and setting aside how their way of operating might be viewed – they continued to use the skills honed in the Lux years, at the 'school' of Gualino. In 1956 the partnership was dissolved and the two producers went their separate ways.[14]

Production details of *The Woman of the River* demonstrate the ways in which the film was shaped by the prevailing market of mid-1950s Italy. Wagstaff (1996: 112) states that in this period income from the home film market was not large enough to cover the costs of production and that, as a result, producers looked to increase profit margins through co-productions (generally within Europe) and through export, with the United States obviously providing the most profitable overseas market. In making this film Ponti sought to draw advantage from following both routes, but his efforts had varying degrees of success. Firstly he packaged and financed it through the co-production funds of Italy (Excelsa/Ponti Cinematografica), and France (Les Films du Centaur) thereby, as in all government-approved co-productions, qualifying for access to two separate sets of national state funding. Secondly, although American funding was not part of the original production costs, it is clear that the film was devised with the export market in mind. Even while production was in progress, the crew openly discussed its similarities with *Bitter Rice* and once it was released it was received by critics as a star vehicle, indeed *the* star vehicle for Loren: the review in *Variety* called it a 'lusty exploitation item which combines elements of such past successes as *Bitter Rice* and *Anna* that will be a natural starrer for Sophia Loren. The US market offers good possibilities if pic is dubbed' (Hawk 1955: 36). The strategy did not entirely pay off. Before Loren secured her Hollywood contract only two of her nationally produced films had been released in America and as we shall see, Loren herself reached Los Angeles and the American public with several other films, long before US distribution of *The Woman of the River*. However, inasmuch as it claimed the attention of Hollywood film-makers looking for new talent in Europe, the film may have contributed to securing Loren's subsequent contract with Stanley Kramer for *The Pride and the Passion* (Masi and Lancia 2004: 65).

The suggestion that this film was a single product that targeted a very particular market must also be qualified if we note that, in 1955, the year following *The Woman of the River*, another film with the same location (the Po delta), the same production company (Ponti Cinematografica, with a French co-producer), the same generic origins (melodrama) and even the same male lead (Rik Battaglia) was released, that is Raffaele Matarazzo's *The Ricefield/La Risaia*, with Elsa Martinelli in the female lead. What is more, budget expenditure for both films was remarkably similar, a fact that somewhat undermines the suggestion that by now the strategy of Ponti's production company was directed solely towards promoting Loren (Appendix B, Archive Sample 2); the casting of Martinelli surely came about largely because she had enjoyed a brief Hollywood career, and was thus known to the international cinema-going public (Buckley 2006: 330). At the very least all this suggests that Loren's role remained only part of an on-going strategy, part of Ponti's various guises as a production company designed to capture international attention and attract funding for future film projects. During the period 1950 to 1955 it is clear that Ponti personally continued to search for a range of talent for the female leads in his films, seen in accounts of the 'discovery' of the Swedish actress May Britt. Reputedly Britt's career began when she was found working in a camera shop during a trip Ponti and Soldati made to Sweden to track down new talent. Her Italian film-making career, though relatively short-lived, shows remarkable parallels with the early film work of Loren herself. She took lead roles in *Jolanda Daughter of the Black Corsair/Jolanda figlia del corsaro nero* (Soldati, 1952), and the opera film *Cavalleria Rusticana* (Gallone, 1953), but only minor parts followed in *The She-Wolf/La lupa* (Lattuada, 1953) and in *War and Peace* (1956), after which she transferred permanently to Hollywood in 1958. This strategy was not uncommon for the period: producers, it is argued, retained a number of starlets in the hope that, sooner or later, one of them might break through to major stardom (Masi and Lancia 2004: 27–8). The place of Ponti in Loren's career trajectory at this time has to be viewed within this wider context, from which it emerges that the Loren–Ponti partnership was only one of several strands to the producer's activities.

Scripting the film

Mario Soldati was both director and scriptwriter for *The Woman of the River*. By 1954 his film-making had been long associated with Ponti, from their already noted first collaboration *Old Fashioned World* in 1940 through a number of successful joint ventures while Ponti worked at Lux. The period of the 1950s is marked by a particular antipathy Soldati showed towards the production team of Ponti–De Laurentiis. It was a collaboration with considerable commercial success but which Soldati seemed to believe did not match what he himself aspired to achieve in his film-making (Farassino 2000: 153–4). Nevertheless, by any standards the scripting of this film was highly problematic. The original idea for the script (*soggetto*) is attributed to Ennio Flaiano and Albero Moravia, but those who wrote the actual script (*sceneggiatura*) are listed as Soldati himself, Antonio Alotoviti, Giorgio Bassani, Pier Paolo Pasolini, Basilio Franchina and Florestano Vancini. In this era it was not at all exceptional to involve multiple scriptwriters but the quality of the listed contributors was without doubt exceptional (Malavisi 2004: 132). While recognizing the particular difficulties of their professional relationship at this time, we can say that Soldati's comments on Ponti's involvement in the script offer interesting insight into the Ponti–Loren film-making process:

> *The Woman of the River* was a dish cooked to a recipe that contained every ingredient imaginable, like a paella from Valencia. [...] Ponti told us that we must have Sophia Loren as the lead and a script containing the following elements: 'you must include a motorbike, a dance, a child that dies, the search for the child that dies; the film must have a sad ending, but it must also have a happy ending, Loren must be in the role of a mother, in the role of an actress, she must be shown riding a bike, Loren must...'. Poor Bassani set himself to script this; he and I tried to pull it together and I must say that despite all these obstacles I think we managed to create some sequences in the film that were well made and convincing. (Malavisi 2004: 131)

These comments are all the more surprising if we note that Ponti was generally regarded as expert at spotting a good script (Cecchi d'Amico 2002: 24). However, some of his greatest successes proved to be found rather in literary sources that he identified as suitable for adapting for the screen: examples would include *The Mill on the Po/Il mulino del Po* (Soldati, 1949) from the novel of Bacchelli, *Two Women* (De Sica, 1960), the film of Moravia's novel *La ciociara*, and the adaptation of Pasternak's *Doctor Zhivago* into the David Lean film of 1965. In this case the strategy of emulating *Bitter Rice* is so explicit as to be counter-productive in that the later film risked negative comparisons with a very remarkable original. The finished film lacked consistent overall tone, oscillating between realism and melodrama, authenticity of location and casting, and explicit foregrounding by the camera of the Loren role. But Soldati is right that it retains some sections of considerable distinction especially in the very fine visuals from the cinematography of Otello Martelli, who went on to work with Fellini on a number of his major films. The slow-paced sequence when Nives and the young girl search for the lost child in the reed-beds is particularly striking as the camera picks out every ripple of the water, ominously suggesting the child's fate. The vistas of the flat, horizonless setting of the Po delta recall the closing sequences of *Ossessione* (Visconti, 1943) and the final episode of *Paisà* (Rossellini, 1946), comparisons certainly to the detriment of the Loren film. However, despite the complex evolution of the script, much of the interest of the film lies in its resultant contradictions, found primarily in the role played by Loren, that of the protagonist Nives, a worker in the local fish factory.

Promoting the film

As well as photo-romances, the cine-romances of the 1950s were also important to Loren's career, no more so than in the cine-romance linked to *The Woman of the River*. As we have seen, the photo-romances played a role that was to an extent tangential to cinema. Clearly the photo-romance had the potential to further a star's career, but it remained a means whereby the reader might independently access and engage with a particular personality that was not directly tied to cinema and the film-making process. The converse was true for the cine-romances, which began publication in 1952. The cine-romances derived directly from cinema, and repeated in a different visual form the narratives of a range of films drawn from national and Hollywood cinema. Publication in Italy ran between 1952 and 1964, and versions were published also in France, Germany and Latin America, where they continued to flourish after cessation of Italian publication (Morreale 2007: 265). One of the main publishers of the cine-romances was Magic Lantern which marketed both the monthly *Cine-romance for All* (*Cineromanzo per tutti*) that combined summaries of film narratives with more general cinema gossip and information; and *Supersize Cine-romance* (*Cineromanzo gigante*) also a monthly publication that consisted almost entirely of the re-presenting of the content of a single film. The owner of Magic Lantern publications was Luigi De Laurentiis, the brother of Dino, and it is therefore not surprising that the series should promote his brother's productions from the years at Ponti–De Laurentiis, and also from their work of earlier years at Lux. The list of films in the *Supersize Cine-romance* (as its title suggests, approximately twice the size of the *Cine-romance for All*) thus includes *La strada* (Fellini, 1954), *Ulysses* (Camerini, 1954) and *War and Peace* (King Vidor, 1956). Three of the editions featured films of Loren: *The White Slave Trade* (with a cover that shows not Loren but the main stars, Eleonora Rossi Drago and Silvana Pampanini), *Attila* (cover showing Loren and co-star Anthony Quinn) and *The Woman of the River* (cover showing Loren alone). There were also covers and full-length versions of the Loren and Mastroianni comedies directed by Blasetti in a separate series entitled *Star Supersize Cine-romances* published by Bozzesi.

All such publications to an extent reinforced the cinematic product, though critics disagree as to whether the public who bought them consisted mainly of confirmed cinema-goers eager to repeat the viewing experience (Morreale 2007: 37), or those unable to access cinema for whom, it is suggested, the magazines were effectively a substitute for the screen version (Amelio 2007: 14). The majority of the magazines were published at any time up to twelve months after the release of the film, though there were also examples from back catalogues of Hollywood and Italy. In this respect the super-size cine-romance of *The Woman of the River* is exceptional because, in contrast, it was published in early October 1954, ahead of the general release of the film itself. This gave the magazine an exceptional place in the marketing strategy of the period, likened to the kind of multimedia blitz associated with more recent times (Morreale 2007: 35). Loren, it seemed, was well placed to benefit from the various strands, visual and written, that Ponti–De Laurentiis had at their disposal to further her career. There is therefore considerable irony in the fact that, despite all efforts to promote Loren and promote the film, it did not achieve the popular success of her other films of the period. In a more general sense we can say that the tradition of cine-romances served to stimulate interest in cinema stars although as with the photo-romance, its significance remains to be fully explored.

Representations of Nives/Loren

The film is perhaps most valuable in its capacity to present, without resolution, the conflicting images of female identity revealed in both the diegetic (the meanings of role of the protagonist) and the extra-diegetic (the meanings of Loren as screen actress/star). The central role in the film offers a spectrum of possible images of Nives, the lead role: a strong independent figure who, in contrast to her fellow-workers resists a submissive demeanour to Gino the male lead; the same independent woman who makes the choice to enter into a relationship with Gino; an apparent reversal as she is then shown as the woman of the home, cooking fish stew (baccalà), while the man comes home from work (admittedly the illicit work of a contraband smuggler); a single mother, deserted by the father who brings up the child on her own, and continues to work to support him; finally, a mother, who loses her child and is united with the father of the child, whom she has betrayed to the police, at the child's funeral. The use of the rural setting may be seen as a trope through which the film raises questions of class and gender more relevant to an evolving, increasingly urban society. As the process of urbanization gathered pace in 1950s Italy, gender roles modified and the tensions resulting from these changes are identifiable as underpinning the text of The Woman of the River. Luisa Cigognetti and Lorenza Servetti show the issue to be fully present in other contemporary media forms. In their analysis of the content, written and visual, of magazines such as Oggi and Epoca in the period 1945–55, they note the 'endless invocation of incompatible role models [...] in newsreels and magazines, where women were praised for their independence while forever condemned to return to their ovens' (1996: 555–6). We will consider firstly how these arguments are realized within the narrative of the film, and then indicate what significance they may have for persona of Loren beyond the text of the individual film.

Commentators are agreed that the meaning of the films of the 'shapely stars' is predicated on the female body (Brunetta 1998: 257–8; Wood 2006: 161). In the case of The Woman of the River one can argue that the film takes as its subject matter precisely the issue of how the camera frames the female body: this leads us in turn to explore the meaning the use of camera gives to the argument of the film. The best evidence for this perspective is found in the central dance sequence that takes place when Nives and her fellow-workers are celebrating at the local village fair. Here, the meaning of the sequence turns on the question of whether the figure of Nives controls or is controlled by the camera's gaze. During the fair Nives excites the attentions of three male admirers, with the male lead Gino in the pivotal role. When Gino arrives, Nives is already in action on the dance floor. We are given a series of point-of-view shots as he stands at the bar watching her. The editing cuts between Gino's look and shots of Nives' body – particularly her upper and lower legs, now revealed, now concealed by her swirling skirt. The scenario is a prime example of the classic Hollywood film that 'places [the woman] in terms of how she may be used for male gratification' (Kaplan 1983: 18). However, these editing conventions and choice of shot are restricted to a brief section of the sequence. The remainder of the sequence and the overall film present the body in a quite different way. Following the encounter with Gino, at the level of narrative, Nives takes control of events. She chooses who to dance with, signalling a freedom to show her body that is reinforced by the different way the camera frames her in relation to those partners. The result is a process that both resists and rejects the objectification proposed by the male (Gino's) gaze.

The second unnamed suitor is from out of town, one of a motorbike gang who in frustration eventually breaks up the community *festa*. His attempts to dance with/court/seduce Nives are rendered comical by the way the camera in all senses makes him look small, showing him from an angle positioned slightly above and behind Loren's shoulder. Here the point-of-view of the camera belongs to Nives, who thus quite literally 'looks down' on him and his arrogant advances. The third admirer, again unnamed, is presented as part of the local community and drawn out of the watching crowd by Nives to dance with her. The camerawork throughout their dance cuts between the couple in a series of medium, medium-long and long shots that give a balanced representation proposing the mutual attraction of their bodies. Without doubt the figure of Nives is more often the focus of the camera, but choice of shot (that is, proximity of the camera to the body) does not otherwise differentiate them. It shows them dancing individually, and performing the dance together so that female and male desire are more evenly and equally delineated on the screen. At this stage of the narrative it may appear that the dramatic interplay of Nives with her other admirers is simply a final but unsuccessful attempt on her part to resist the charms of Gino. However, a different and much more valid meaning can be established if we interpret the dance episode in conjunction with the final sequence of the film.

A significant argument on the films of this era states that in their display of the body, the body of the 'shapely star', the films are informed by a sense of 'Catholic sinfulness, passion and mortification' (Brunetta 1998: 256): these are elements that in any case are commonly associated with the genre form to which this film belongs, the melodrama. As the narrative progresses, it appears to suggest the logic that Nives, as transgressive woman, is punished when her child drowns in the river. However, this interpretation is countered by the construction of the final lengthy sequence of the film depicting the child's funeral procession. Here it becomes clear that the 'punishment' of the female is shared by Gino and accompanying members of the community. As the sequence opens Nives is located centrally, the local community surrounding and moving forward with her. Gino stands separate on the margins with a police guard, but he then joins her, as if to share punishment for the 'sin'. As a couple they now remain part of the communal mourning procession right up to the film's final shot. The supposedly sinful woman is neither marginalized nor excluded from her fellow rural workers, represented as a unified group moving forward together to an indeterminate future. As we saw in Soldati's summary of the 'Valencian paella' that was the scripting of *The Woman of the River*, the dance sequence was a necessary ingredient, at the very least because it thus echoed the famous boogie-woogie dance of Silvana Mangano in *Bitter Rice*. The fortunes of the female protagonist in the two films are however quite different. The Mangano character, also called Silvana, betrays her fellow-workers and finally makes reparation by taking her own life. The workers move towards her inert body to sprinkle it with rice, suggesting they still see her as one of their own. But clearly Silvana is punished for the trangressive quality of her role, located ostensibly in the deception she plays on the other rice-pickers. Implicitly, and more accurately however, it is the voluptuous seductiveness of her body that results in a standard conclusion to the melodrama, the marginalization or exclusion of the sinful female. Instead, *The Woman of the River* argues forcefully for the inclusion of Nives, and the assertive sexuality her role encompasses, as integral to the future society represented in the final shots of the film.

Reception of the film

The Woman of the River premiered in Italy in December 1954, and went on general release in Italy early in the following year. It was released in the United States in September 1957, by which time American audiences had already been given the opportunity to view Loren in two Italian films and three runaway productions, details of which will be more fully explored in Chapter 3. In terms of box-office success, the period 1954–6 marks the high point of Loren's early career: 1954–5 was dubbed 'the year of Sophia' because four of her films figured in the annual listing of the most successful national films (*The Gold of Naples, Neapolitan Carousel, Too Bad She's Bad* and *The Sign of Venus*), and figures for 1955–6 show that the momentum was maintained with three further films in the highest-grossing category, *Scandal in Sorrento, The Miller's Beautiful Wife* and *Lucky to Be a Woman* (Bernardi 2002: 659–61). The one very marked absence from the grouping is precisely *The Woman of the River*, reinforcing the argument of an early critical review that 'a film aimed at creating or consolidating a star image is not so easy [...] and as far as the image of Sophia Loren is concerned, this film has been only partially successful in contributing to that process' (Marinucci 1955: 12). In terms of constructing Loren's persona, then, what is the significance of the film? It is valuable to attempt an answer in relation to how the film might have been received by a contemporary audience. At this point in her career Loren remained very closely associated with the character of Donna Sofia, the pizza-seller of *The Gold of Naples*. It was a role perceived as attractive and typical of the spontaneous popular world (Gundle 1995: 371), qualities that were then quickly associated with Loren herself. To an extent the actress's image was conflated with her on-screen role to create a single, uncomplicated image of female identity. As her career progressed it is clear that audiences largely preferred to consume the product that was Sophia Loren through her roles in comedy films. The role of Nives raises more explicit questions about female sexuality and as such gives a clearer indication of the social transitions evolving in postwar Italy. It was a role that, additionally, linked more directly into the powerful sexuality, the potentially subversive qualities of Loren herself. As we have seen, hers was a physicality that beauty competition judges were unwilling to acknowledge with their main awards. Although *The Woman of the River* is a film with many weaknesses, its commercial fortunes suggest that the audience was also resistant to a film role that did not marry with that of the simple Neapolitan girl, the popular image of Loren already in vogue through her other contemporary films. As subsequent chapters will show, these contradictions, and the complexities of reconciling on- and off-screen images, were to persist in the continuing process of constructing Loren's star identity.

Notes

1. The troubled history of Loren and her family is very fully covered in the biographies of Warren Harris (1980) and Italo Moscati (2005). On Riccardo Scicolone, Sophia's father, see especially chapters entitled 'Sophia Toothpick' (Harris 1980: 15–24), and 'The Seducer (Il seduttore)' (Moscati 2005: 41–52).

2. As a number of commentators have noted, it was a label first used in Blasetti's film In Olden Times/ Altri tempi (1952). In the episode 'The Frine Trial (Il processo di frine)', Vittorio De Sica plays the part of a defence lawyer whose address to the court describes the defendant, played by Gina Lollobrgida, as 'una maggiorata fisica'. The term was then applied, in the plural maggiorate fisiche, to the whole grouping of which Lollobrigida, Mangano, Loren and others were a part. I have amended the rather lengthy literal translation, 'physically well-endowed stars', to 'shapely stars', and will use this translation throughout the book.

3. Shortly after, the periodical published a letter of response from Lollobrigida where she accused Callari of being ill-informed on the matter. In her most recent success, The Wayward Wife/La provinciale (Soldati, 1953), for which she received a Best Actress award, she assures him that it is her voice that is used. The further accusation, that the jury was biased because one of its members, Alberto Moravia was also the scriptwriter of the films is also refuted: Moravia, she states, informed the jury of this possible conflict of interest and abstained from participating in the vote that awarded her the prize (Lollobrigida 1953: 3).

4. In his very rich study of the relationship between the United States and another European nation, Spain, Rosendorf takes the argument further to suggest that US cinema links to Europe may be interpreted also as a form of 'soft power', a means of implicitly exerting influence in a part of the world with increasing strategic importance as the Cold War asserted itself in the 1950s (Rosendorf 2007: 78). Babington and Evans (1993) interpret the biblical epics, many of which were filmed in Europe, as a trope that articulated the US aspiration towards cultural and political primacy in the area.

5. For a full account of the documentation the producer was required to submit see Appendix A.

6. Details of the content of the 1949 laws is set out in Quaglietti (1974), in which he also provides a very valuable summary of the context, political and cultural from which they emerged. For an example of what might be termed 'self-regulation' on the part of producers, see Marcus's careful study of the scripting of Bread, Love and Dreams (Comencini, 1953) (Marcus 1986: 122–43); for an example of what is claimed to be direct censorship, see director Giuseppe De Santis's own account of his unsuccessful attempts to make a film entitled Noi che facciamo crescere il grano about the brutal government treatment of workers' unrest in Calabria, Southern Italy (Parigi 1986: 31–34). The 'De Santis case' is fully explored in an unpublished thesis by Paolo Russo (1993). It is also worth mentioning the on-going project on the subject by a number of Italian researchers including Tatti Sanguineti and Pier Luigi Raffaelli entitled, 'Italia Taglia' which in 1999 mounted an exhibition and published a first volume of findings edited by Tatti Sanguineti.

7. According to Ruffin (2002: 277) it is unclear whether Rosa Film was run by Ponti alone, or in conjunction with De Laurentiis. Bernardini (2000: 371) lists the directors of Rosa Film as Antonio Altoviti, Vincenzo Cossa, Luigi De Laurentiis and Mario Perelli, and identifies Luigi De Laurentiis, the brother of Dino, as director of productions. Ponti himself gives an account of the marketing strategies he used to generate the substantial profits he made on the Totò films (Della Casa 2003: 231)

8. The details set out in this chapter for Lux and Titanus refer specifically to the mode of production in the years of Loren's early film career. By the early 1960s Titanus had scaled down the scope of its operations, and functioned mainly as a distributor – for films such as Loren's *Two Women/La ciociara* (De Sica, 1960) and *Rocco and his Brothers/Rocco e i suoi fratelli* (Visconti, 1960). Following a period of loss-making productions in the mid-fifties, of which *The Wayward Countess/Senso* (Visconti, 1954) is the most frequently cited example, Lux also gradually withdrew from its role as a production company. This chapter concentrates on the role of the companies broadly with regard to the role they played in the careers of Loren and Ponti. The fullest account of the very substantial contribution they made to postwar Italian filmmaking is found in two publications on Titanus, by Barlozetti (1980) and Bernardini (1986); and the late Alberto Farassino's publications on Lux, one co-authored with Tatti Sanguineti (1984) and a later single-authored edition (2000). I have drawn extensively on this material, and supplemented it with evidence from the film files of the Central State Archive. Brunetta (1998) also analyses the role of Lux, and there are short resumes of the work of both studios in the cinema history series of the National Film School published by Marsilio. Full publication details are listed in the main bibliography: specific points from individual texts are individually referenced.

9. Of the two studio heads, Goffredo Lombardo was the more suited to public relations and quite clearly the more alert to the importance of promoting his company. Bernardini's history of the studio includes examples of detailed brochures, published by the studio, aimed at engaging the public's interest and understanding of how Titanus ran its business. The character of Riccardo Gualino, by nature a much more reserved, rather distant individual, set a different tone to activities in the Lux studio. It was his son Renato who became the public face of the studio, and who was for several years president of the National Producers Association, part of ANICA. On the international stage in the 1950s Renato Gualino was also president of the US branch of the Italian Film Export Association (IFE), which interacted – perhaps rather too closely, as Wagstaff (1996: 106) suggests – with the operations of Lux itself.

10. A range of figures are available to indicate the tenuous nature of film production work in Italy. Quaglietti (1974) presents figures that show that in the period 1945–1958, 463 companies were in production, of which 287 produced only a single film. Bernardini's figures (2000: XIII) show that such a profile was not unique to the immediate postwar era. In his survey for the wider period 1930–1995, he shows that 2,912 films were produced, 1,802 of which were the only product made by the listed production company.

11. The distinction between 'public' and 'private' becomes somewhat blurred when we take into account the fact that, rather than giving actual cash advances to producers, distributors often provided instead credit documents (*cambiali*) with which producers could obtain credit from the BNL (Banca Nazionale del Lavoro), the institution that was also the source of direct government grants. However, the distributor remained ultimately responsible for repaying the loan, a fact that counted heavily against Titanus, when it later sustained heavy losses in the funding of films such as *Sodom and Gomorrah* (Aldrich, 1963). For further discussion of the funding of this film see Chapter 5.

12. Fuller information on the Italian Actors Union can be found on the archive website listed in the bibliography, a valuable source of written and photographic materials that record the activities of the union since its formation in April 1960. The absence of an actors' organization is very simply evidenced in the annual report on Italian cinema for 1955 supplied to the trade publication *Film Daily Yearbook* of 1956. Throughout the 1950s the report was supplied by Eitel Monaco, the

president of ANICA or *Associazione Nazionale Industrie Cinematografiche ed Affini* (National Association of Motion Pictures and Allied Industries). The report identifies the groups that ANICA represents as: National Association of Film Producers; National Association of Film Distributors; National Association of Film Technicians; National Association of Sub-Standard-Width Motion Pictures; and AGIS, the association of exhibitors (Monaco 1958: 616). The one glaring omission from the list is of course a grouping of any sort capable of representing the actors themselves.

13. A full understanding of the significance of the photo-romances is difficult, particularly because of problems with availability of material. Only Universo, the publisher of *Grand Hotel* holds a stock of past titles. Otherwise, back copies of *Sogno* and *Bolero Film* can be traced only in private collections, and this is the case also with the cine-romances (for this study I used originals from the private collection of Mina Fabbri). Two recent exhibitions have gone some way to facilitating access to this material: the Sophia Loren exhibition at the Museo Vittoriano in Rome in May 2006, and the other 'Cinema on the Page: History and Stories of the Cine-romances' at the National Museum of Cinema of Turin in March 2007, largely based on the private collection of the film director Gianni Amelio). Both exhibitions have published catalogues with samples of the materials displayed at the exhibitions. The second difficulty lies in the fact that there is insufficient data available to establish a clear understanding of the patterns of consumption of the photo-romances and the cine-romances. Bravo cites weekly circulation figures in the 1950s of 1,000,000 for *Grand Hotel* and 600,000 for *Sogno* and *Bolero Film* (Bravo 2003: 21): however Morreale emphasizes that evidence of the type of reader who bought the magazines is almost non-existent because marketing surveys such as readership take-up by location, class or gender were rarely adopted in this early period of circulation (2007: 37). Both critics underline the importance of developing this area of research in order to enhance our understanding of the role these publications played in postwar Italian culture.

14. As with the history of Lux and Titanus, it is only possible here to summarize briefly the work of Ponti and De Laurentiis. Fuller details are found in the cited studio histories, in Stefano Della Casa's *Capitani coraggiosi* (2003) and in relevant sections of the Marsilio publications on the history of the industry edited by the National Film School. There is also a monograph of the career of De Laurentiis by Tullio Kezich and Alessandra Levantesi (2003).

3

Loren and Hollywood

Sophia goes to Hollywood

In September 1955 Sophia Loren completed filming for *Lucky to Be a Woman*. The film was well received by critics and the public: it was first screened in Rome in December and, as we saw in Chapter 2, had a spectacular premiere in early 1956 during the Winter Olympics in the Italian Dolomites, an event that underlined Loren's status as an established, popular national star. From this point on, until she began work on *Two Women/La ciociara* (De Sica, 1960) in September 1960, she began her 'Hollywood years', a period that has been largely overlooked, given scant attention by commentators who focus on her career in Italy and her place in Italian culture as the main point of reference. However, her involvement in the Hollywood film industry is in fact the decisive factor in establishing what might be called her 'super-stardom', when she moves from limited national acclaim to the monopoly status of *the* Italian icon. Loren eventually achieved international stardom, but the process was neither straightforward (there was no simple progression from Italian to Hollywood acclaim) nor without some very substantial changes in her personal life. Dyer stresses promotion and publicity as central to constructing the star image, and the chapter case study demonstrates the very particular role these categories played in Loren's career during this period (Dyer 1998: 60–1). In the early years of her film-making, Loren was given the standard press treatment of all Italian 'shapely stars'. With the Hollywood contract, Loren crossed continents not only geographically, but also cinematically and culturally. To understand fully her career progress it is important to emphasize this very changed agenda, and to identify the ways in which her evolving persona was presented in Italy and internationally, on screen and in the press. During the Hollywood years her professional career became almost engulfed by the media attention given to her personal life. Carlo Ponti obtained a divorce from his first wife Giuliana Fiastri and in September 1957, he and Loren entered into a proxy marriage in Mexico that was subsequently declared bigamous by the Italian authorities. In the high level of publicity that followed, her on-screen achievements became almost secondary to her off-screen persona, a characteristic that has been noted in the career paths of other pin-up stars of the period, Marilyn Monroe and Rita

Hayworth being prime examples, as well as secondary figures such as Diana Dors and Jayne Mansfield (Cook 2001: 169). We shall see that the term 'the Hollywood years' is in many ways a blanket term of convenience that covers a complex phase of adjustment and alteration in Loren's public and personal life, elements that converged to forge for her a different form of stardom.

Figure 1: Sophia, dressed by Emile Schuberth, preparing for departure to Hollywood April 1957. Stills Department, Cineteca Nazionale, Rome.

Under the heading 'Sophia Loren goes to Hollywood' (Anon (b) 1957: 137) the international press carried carefully staged shots of the actress, set to make her journey in an elegant dress designed for her by couturier Emile Schuberth. The label on her enormous packing cases, 'Sophia Loren, Hollywood', is just visible in the shot (Figure 1). A separate pose showed her, tearful and suitably apprehensive, looking out the window of a plane about to take off from Rome airport. On 8 April 1957 the plane touched down in Los Angeles, where she was to take up a major contract with Paramount Pictures, but in a number of ways Loren's career was marked by the influence of Hollywood well before this date. In the broadest sense Hollywood had been a major influence in Italy (and in Europe more generally) since the end of the Second World War, with regard to the uptake of American films by European audiences, and then additionally through American funding of European film-making. American influence was central to the cultural re-formation of postwar Europe, as a number of studies have shown (Ellwood and Brunetta 1991; Nowell-Smith 1998). The United States was keen to re-establish Europe as a market for their films: in the case of Italy American films had been absent not just during the war period, but since 1938, when protectionist measures taken by the fascist authorities brought about the withdrawal of the main Hollywood distributors from the Italian market.[1] American capital contributed directly to the postwar Italian film industry: under the terms of the Andreotti Law a percentage of profits made on American films was retained in Italy, and the American majors channelled these 'frozen' funds into Italian film-making in a number of ways. Firstly there were the 'runaway productions' where stars and director were US-based, and the Italians supplied technical support and locations (often the externals of Rome and the studio space of Cinecittà). Examples of this include *Three Coins in the Fountain* (Negulesco, 1953), produced by Twentieth Century Fox and MGM's *Ben Hur* (Wyler, 1960). In such cases funding was the responsibility of the relevant American major. Alternatively, in a process termed 'compartecipazione', American profits retained in Italy were used as part-payment for productions that also qualified as 'national Italian' making them eligible for the various preferential loans and grants available from national government funds. Cast and technical crew were Italian, and profits were shared between the Italian and American financiers.

The term 'compartecipazione' is most easily translated as a form of 'American co-production', but it differed from a 'European co-production' in a number of significant ways. Within Europe the making of joint films was governed by a series of reciprocal agreements that implied a relationship of parity between the participating parties, and functioned to their mutual benefit. Italy and France worked regularly together in this way: as both were subsidised industries, Franco-Italian co-productions films qualified for support from the separate national governments. European productions of this type are extensively documented, enabling us to have a clear understanding of the detail of the process. In contrast deals were struck between the majors and Italian production companies in piecemeal fashion for single film projects only: this was the case with some of Loren's own films, and several production arrangements of the Ponti–De Laurentiis company. Documentation on these public-private deals must have been submitted to the relevant authorities but it seems that the papers concerning the US input were treated as just so, that is private, and not available to public scrutiny. Archive files include only the papers relevant to the Italian part of the production package, and this makes it more difficult to trace fully the uses of US monies in the Italian film market. A third, alternative scenario was also possible, where the majors input funds at a later stage, at the point when international distribution rights were negotiated. Guback argues that in such cases, which he terms 'pickup deals', it becomes almost impossible to be clear about the original source of the film's funding (Guback 1976: 401–2). Loren's films provide examples of this varied range of production arrangements, and the relevance of these issues to her career path will be considered in the course of the chapter.

Sophia Loren's image had already been present in the American market for some considerable time before film contracts were signed. However, when her face started to become familiar to the American public it was not through the moving image, the wide diffusion of her Italian films, but instead through the circulation of stills in promotional exposés, magazine covers and pin-up shots. In the 1950s the American press was particularly diligent in seeking out and circulating images of potential new European stars. Thus on 22 August 1955 Loren made the first (of seven) career appearances on the cover of *Life* magazine, in a shot from her role as Donna Sofia, the fish-seller in *Scandal in Sorrento/Pane amore e...*(1955).[2] The emphasis of the accompanying single-page article is interesting. It implied that Hollywood was only now catching up with a star already well known to European audiences, showing twelve sample covers from German, Swiss, French, English and Italian publications to make the point that 'Sophia Loren has become the Continent's foremost cover girl' and concludes that 'with this issue she at last makes her appearance on the cover of *Life*' (Anon (c) 1955: 42). There was of course a long tradition of European stars relocating to Hollywood, a history that stretches from the careers of Valentino and Garbo in the silent era to the present. Sustaining a non-Hollywood cinematic discourse, and particularly a non-Hollywood cinematic industry, has been consistently problematic for national film industries and their stars. However, this was a period of particular crisis in the American film industry which had driven producers to look to Europe for fresh audiences and as a location for runaway productions. For Loren and the Hollywood film industry, there was reciprocal advantage in her featuring on the cover of *Life*. A new face could boost magazine sales; more importantly it introduced the actress to a new market, while for Hollywood it offered the potential to boost flagging box-office revenues.

In the late 50s still shots (pin-up poses, press photos at festivals and film premieres, magazine 'photo-galleries') remained virtually the only visual means beyond the films themselves that offered the public access to the star. Most prominently of all, the 1950s were 'the glory years of photography' that marked the career of Marilyn Monroe, but this era was brought to a close by changes in technology, specifically the use of video, used to record events such as the Kennedy presidency of the early 1960s (Woodward 2002: 33). The drive by the star and those promoting the star to draw maximum advantage from circulating the photographic image was relentless, and in any field of entertainment this is to be expected. But in the mid-1950s Hollywood's search for non-American stars was particularly marked, as the film market struggled to retain the advantage over the growing popularity of television. Even before Loren's plane touched down, *Variety* was recording advance publicity for another shapely star, Brigitte Bardot, whose film *God Created Woman/Et Dieu créa la femme* (Vadim, 1956) was due for US release, noting that 'very erotic poses of her are circulating in advance' (Hift 1957: 95). Throughout 1957 *Photoplay* showbiz correspondent Sidney Skolsky made repeated reference to Bardot in his weekly trivia column 'That's Hollywood!', indicating that 'sexy pics are in circulation' that suggest 'Bardot will be the next big European sensation' (Skolsky 1957: 24). Finally, as Loren left Italy for Hollywood, Hollywood in turn remained a particularly strong presence in Italy where 'Hollywood by the Tiber' – the coming of American stars (Ava Gardner, Tyrone Power, Gregory Peck, Orson Welles) to film in Rome – combined with a burgeoning Italian economy and more affluent lifestyle of Vespas and fashion to put the image of a glamorous Italy on display. A degree of cross-fertilization is apparent: to an extent Loren re-exported this aura of glamour back to Hollywood.

Runaway productions

Loren's Hollywood career had two distinct phases. It began with individual contracts for three productions shot in Europe, each in a different location, each with major Hollywood leads cast as Loren's co-stars. This was followed by a package-deal with Paramount Pictures that began in Los Angeles and concluded in Europe. The first group of European-based productions include three films:

1. *The Pride and the Passion*: externals shot in Spain, production completed in Los Angeles; directed by Stanley Kramer; produced by Stanley Kramer productions, distributed by United Artists; co-stars Cary Grant and Frank Sinatra.
2. *Boy on a Dolphin*: externals shot in Greece, production completed at Cinecittà; directed by Jean Negulesco; produced and distributed by Twentieth Century Fox, co-stars Alan Ladd and Clifton Webb.
3. *Legend of the Lost*: externals shot in Libya, production completed at Cinecitta; directed by Henry Hathaway; produced by Batjac/Dear Films, distributed by United Artists, co-stars John Wayne and Rossano Brazzi.

Because of the distant locations used, the crews of these 'runaway productions' were almost entirely American. Concerns regarding the impact of runaway productions were repeatedly reflected both in correspondence from trades unions, and in the film press, with a range of conflicting views clearly in evidence.[3] Within Italy controversy surrounding the funding of *Legend of the Lost* showed the dilemma of European governments allocating funds in a subsidised industry that raised the question, to what extent should a national government support financially what was effectively an American production? The Loren film involved only three weeks shooting and editing in Rome, with the remainder of the filming scheduled to take place in Libya (ACS/PL/*Legend of the Lost*). Production details like this show that the label of 'American co-production' with a European partner might contribute little in the way of profits or employment to the relevant national industry. Despite this, the producers secured government approval and funding for *Legend of the Lost*: it was awarded 'minority national status' on the grounds that, 'the present situation in the film industry makes is essential that we support projects that provide employment for our workers' (ACS/MV/*Legend of the Lost*).[4] Loren's next film, *The Pride and the Passion*, marked a further departure from the input of Italy to runaway productions in the early years of the decade. Stanley Kramer was one of the first directors to negotiate with the Franco regime for shooting rights in Spain; as such the film began a shift to use Spanish locations and extras where producers were able to negotiate costs at a lower level than they incurred in Italy (Guback 1969: 401). Spanish locations featured also in Loren's later work, *El Cid* (1962) and *The Fall of the Roman Empire* (1964), both directed by Anthony Mann, and thereafter they were to become the setting most commonly associated with Sergio Leone's low-budget Spaghetti Westerns, filmed in the Almeria countryside. Use of Spanish locations became increasingly widespread: British film-maker David Lean found them ideal for the desert sequences of *Lawrence of Arabia* (1962) and, most remarkably, he used the buildings of Seville to double for Moscow in the later *Doctor Zhivago* (1965). With this phase of film-making concluded, Loren secured a contract with Paramount Pictures and transferred to Hollywood where she made four films: *Desire under the Elms* (Delbert Mann, 1957), *Houseboat* (Shavelson, 1958), *The Black Orchid* (Ritt, 1958) and *That Kind of Woman* (Lumet, 1959). The remaining three films of the Paramount deal were *Heller in Pink Tights* (Cukor, 1960) and *A Breath of Scandal* (Curtiz, 1960) that both involved European location shooting, while the last, *It Started in Naples* (Shavelson, 1960) was shot entirely on location in Italy.

The Paramount connection

Initial reports of Loren's Paramount contract suggested a most remarkable deal had been struck. Her second cover appearance in *Life* on 6 May 1957 was reinforced by an article that termed her the '$3 million bambina', stating that she had received $200,000 for each of the three runaway productions she had already completed, to which would now be added the sum of £2 million for the Hollywood package: with the possibility of a percentage share of the profits, *Life* said this was 'the biggest deal [...] that any import ever landed in movie history' (Anon (b) 1957: 137). Though the deal itself may be seen as exceptional, the fact that an Italian star was linked to a Paramount contract is not so remarkable if we consider again the situation of Italo-American film-making in the postwar period, when Hollywood sought to re-establish its market in Europe. Brunetta states that by September 1945 eight US majors – Twentieth Century Fox, MGM, Universal, Columbia, Paramount, RKO, Warner Bothers and United Artists had re-established an Italian base, each with a nominated representative in place (Brunetta 1998: 654). The representative for Paramount Films of Italy was Pilade Levi. He originally served as a US army captain during the period of the liberation and was listed as a member of the film board that met in Rome in June 1944: the board, led by Admiral Stone of Allied Command, was set up in liberated Rome to consider how the national film industry might be managed in the post-fascist era (Quaglietti 1974: 3).[5] Thus the US army captain remained in Italy, and became civilian Pilade Levi, head of Paramount Films of Italy in September 1945. The company became heavily involved in a number of Italo-American film-making ventures, including *Mambo* (Rosen, 1954), *Ulysses* (Camerini, 1955) and *War and Peace* (King Vidor, 1956).

Most importantly, Paramount undertook extensive co-production activity with the Ponti–De Laurentiis production company, a commercial relationship that eventually offered potential connections for Sophia Loren's individual career. The film *The Brigand Musolino/Il brigante Musolino* (Camerini, 1950) starring Silvana Mangano and Amedeo Nazzari was the first Ponti–De Laurentiis production and Ponti proudly proclaimed it also to be 'the first film made in Italy with American money' (Farassino and Sanguineti 1984: 300). Ponti makes clear that, in partnership with Paramount's Pilade Levi, they planned another 25 films with similar funding arrangements, but instead *The Brigand Musolino* proved to be both the first and last film in a long-term project that was still-born.[6] He and De Laurentiis continued a form of partnership with Paramount whereby a range of different production deals were struck. In 1950s Italy a fully reciprocal relationship between the Italian and the American film industries was for a long time the goal, particularly pursued through the very enthusiastic efforts of Eitel Monaco, head of the Italian producers association ANICA. Corsi terms it a goal that was to remain little more than a 'mirage'. A single major agreement of this nature was not forthcoming because, she argues, the American industry resisted any attempt to yield its dominant position, maintaining thereby that Italy was never more than a junior partner in Hollywood's international undertakings (Corsi 2001: 70). Given that this was broadly the position also for other European film industries, the very fact that Ponti and De Laurentiis regularly secured US funding counts in itself as a considerable achievement.

Both in their work at Lux, and with their own production company Ponti and De Laurentiis were the producers seen as most orientated towards Hollywood practices, for their commitment to creating stars and to making films that were star vehicles, and also for their success in attracting American funding. The connection to Paramount formed a major part of their production activity, but it does not follow that Loren's international contract would necessarily be with this particular studio. All the evidence shows that Loren was destined for a Hollywood career in some form, and we must remember that her first three 'Hollywood' films involved deals with US majors other than Paramount. Before this major contract was confirmed *The New York Times* had also reported that she was to be the lead in two films planned by the American independent company Hecht-Lancaster, but the project did not come to fruition (Pryor 1956: 22). As noted in Chapter 2, when Ponti operated within the Ponti–De Laurentiis production company his aim to further Loren's career was only one of a range of projects and possible star careers to which he was committed. Once the partners separated, in a number of ways De Laurentiis continued to pursue his aspirations to work on the Hollywood scale:[7] Ponti instead retained his business interests in Europe – largely through the new production company Champion – but from this time on his American-orientated activities concentrated largely on achieving and managing international success for Loren. We cannot know the precise details of how Loren's Hollywood contract came about. The connections between Paramount and Ponti–De Laurentiis are without doubt of prime significance, and one might legitimately speculate that through his close industry links to Paramount Ponti increasingly negotiated for himself the role of an astute agent for Loren. However, it is important to emphasize that the Paramount–Loren agreement did not take place in isolation, but instead emerged from roots also traceable in the wider interaction of the contemporary Italian and American film industries.

The Paramount contracts

Loren's link to Paramount eventually came about through not one, but several contracts. The first, with the conditions cited from *Life* magazine, was subsequently termed a 'personal-employment contract' to differentiate it from the other contractual arrangements that followed (Pryor 1957b: 27). The personal-employment contract was short-lived, and, after the making of *Desire under the Elms* and *Houseboat*, was superseded by two further deals. These required her participation as main actor, but this time Paramount drew up contracts not with Loren herself but with Carlo Ponti and Marcello Girosi whom they employed as producers in a two-picture deal to make *The Black Orchid* (1958) and *That Kind of Woman* (1959) (Pryor 1957b: 29); and then in a later, second deal to produce *Heller in Pink Tights* (1960) and *A Breath of Scandal* (1960) (Pryor 1959: 21). The terms of the initial contract clearly did not tie Loren exclusively to Paramount: she was free to make other films at the time and after *Desire under the Elms* she went to England to make *The Key*, a Columbia-funded film with co-stars William Holden and Trevor Howard. At a time when the contracts of all stars, American and European, were moving to freelance status, there was wide variation in the terms and conditions governing their work that strongly influenced individual career trajectories. It is commonplace to gauge star qualities in relative terms; in the case of the 'shapely stars' this often worked at the most banal level of comparing vital statistics. Press reports compared Loren's measurements to her Italian counterparts (Lollobrigida and Mangano) at first, and then later to those of Hollywood stars and starlets (Marilyn Monroe and Jayne Mansfield). It is much more pertinent, and in a different sense much more revealing, to compare conditions of employment, where radical differences become apparent. The 1950s was a period of great social transition, but it was also a time of transition in the film industry, particularly the Hollywood film industry, and this is reflected in the very different contractual conditions that impacted on the career of a number of stars contemporaneous with Loren.

As in the case of Loren, Hollywood had broadcast the anticipated career prospects of Gina Lollobrigida with a fanfare of publicity. Such was Lollobrigida's popularity that she effectively became the face of Italian cinema on the covers of *Life* and *Time* and took on the role of a kind of ambassador for Italian cinema in the early part of the decade, attending promotional events (international premieres and film weeks organized by IFE, the Italian Film Export association) in London and Washington.[8] Despite this, for her a US film career never fully materialised. In 1950, after discussions with the head of studio Howard Hughes she signed a seven-year contract with RKO. Hughes' eccentric mode of operating eventually brought about the collapse of the entire RKO company: as for Lollobrigida, her contract excluded her from working with any other major US production company, but at the same time RKO failed to initiate any film projects for her. She quickly abandoned Hollywood and returned to Europe where she made a number of highly successful Franco–Italian co-productions *Fanfan la tulipe* (Christian-Jacque, 1952) and *Beauties of the Night/Les belles de nuit* (Clair, 1952) as well as taking the lead in the high-grossing *Bread and Love* series. The popularity of these films made 1953–4 'the year of Gina' at the Italian box office. She returned briefly to US film-making in the late 50s, but by then other stars – such as Loren and Brigitte Bardot – and other events had eclipsed her Hollywood prospects. In this respect she was one of a long line of Italian stars from Alida Valli to Pier Angeli whose Hollywood experience ended in failure.[9] Contractual problems of this nature were not restricted to non-American stars. Marilyn Monroe's difficulties with Twentieth Century Fox have been widely documented. In 1950 she entered into a seven-year contract but by the mid-1950s found the conditions too restrictive, and refused parts she considered unsuited to the major star status she had by then achieved. For a time she formed her own production company, Marilyn Monroe Productions, that co-produced two further films in which she took lead roles *Bus Stop* (Logan, 1956) and *The Prince and the Showgirl* (Olivier, 1957).

It is interesting to note the approach of stars newer to the Hollywood industry where it becomes clear that within the span of a few years, the handling of star contracts made the most rapid changes.[10] In the post-studio regime actors might negotiate individually with the studios, but more commonly they relied on the skills of an agent. In his very brief time as a star, James Dean was renowned for his resistance to studio pressures. After the success in *East of Eden* (Kazan, 1954) he had, through his agent, negotiated a film-by-film deal that also allowed him to work in television where his career began. This was further evidence that the 'old school' had to bow to the pressures of the new star power by allowing flexibility of employment agreements (Gomery 2005: 185). The changes to Loren's conditions of employment certainly suggest a weakening of her status within the industry. The inclusion of Ponti and Girosi in the contracts offers the distinct appearance of a strategy designed to bale out the less-than-glorious progress of her Hollywood films but, as we shall see, their participation did little to halt Loren's struggling fortunes. Despite these adjustments, the links with Paramount remained crucial to moulding her Hollywood career. In contrast to Monroe, Lollobrigida and other aspiring emigrés actors, the contracts gave flexibility that enabled her eventually to extricate herself from a faltering career path that was revived again from within Europe.

Films in America/American films
Phillips and Vincendeau have extensively summarized the great number of European emigrés who undertook what they term the 'journey of desire' to Hollywood (2006: 17). The availability and distribution of Loren's films raise a question fundamental to the evolving of her international persona. Industry records show that prior to her plane landing in Los Angeles, virtually none of her films had been seen by the American public. The runaway productions were yet to be released, and only two of her Italian films had been screened in America – *Aida* and *Too Bad She's Bad*. The summary of her US releases at this crucial time is as follows:[11]

Film title	Production company/year of production		US release date
Aida	Oscar Film	1953	October 1954
Too Bad She's Bad	Documento Film	1954	Dec 1955
The Gold of Naples	Ponti–De Laurentiis	1954	February 1957
Boy on a Dolphin	Twentieth Century Fox	1957	April 1957
Scandal in Sorrento	Titanus	1955	May 1957
The Miller's Beautiful Wife	Ponti–De Laurentiis	1955	June 1957
The Pride and the Passion	Stanley Kramer Productions	1957	July 1957
The Woman of the River	Ponti–De Laurentiis	1955	Sept. 1957
Legend of the Lost	Batjac/Dear Film	1957	Dec. 1957

Sources: *Motion Picture Almanac* 1957/1958; *Film Daily Year Book* 1957/1958.

A number of important points emerge from this listing. In general there was often a considerable time lapse in Italian films reaching the United States. The list shows for example that *The Gold of Naples* (and even other great popular successes like *Bread, Love and Dreams*) did not quickly command the attention of American distributors. Neither was it unknown for a European star to arrive in Hollywood ahead of the release of his/her successful indigenous films. When Marlene Dietrich's first Hollywood film Morocco (Von Sternberg, 1930) premiered in the American market, The Blue Angel (Von Sternberg, 1930), her great European success had still to be released. Publicity for Morocco made a play precisely on this point, promising that the film would 'now, for the first time' give them the opportunity to experience directly the allure of a new, much-anticipated star (Ellis 1982: 24). For Loren, 1957 was marked by successive premieres for her completed runaway productions, and to these was added the release of a backlog of material clearly aimed at capitalizing on her anticipated popularity. The above figures make quite clear that a substantial body of raw material – in short Loren's Italian films – played almost no part at all in creating her image ahead of her arrival in the United States. Philips and Vincendeau suggest that the so-called journey of desire is 'bound up with the myth of reinventing oneself' (2006: 17). Since US audiences were largely unfamiliar with her earlier work, one can argue that assessment of her Hollywood potential rested largely with producers and distributors who believed that Sophia Loren, and Sophia Loren's films, would be popular, revenue-generating products. The process of constructing Loren's Hollywood stardom did not therefore involve renegotiating established public perception of an established star. It was located rather at the level of production, where film-makers took on the task of fashioning a potential star career for a new, largely untried audience.

On the first level, transfer to Hollywood presented all emigrés with some very specific difficulties. Under the heading 'Language and Performance' Philips and Vincendeau argue that language problems (identified as accent, comprehensibility, the effort of linking overall performance – body language, facial expression – to unfamiliar verbal expression), were contributory factors to the 'floundering' of the careers of several European stars, citing Marcello Mastroianni, and Alain Delon as examples (2006: 10–12). However, one cannot be categorical about this issue: a strong accent might pose the obstacle to a star's success, but in the case of Dietrich and Maurice Chevalier, the opposite was true. But the question of 'comprehensibility' goes beyond a grasp of simple turns of phrase to mean understanding the nuances of speech and gesture as they transfer across the different cultures. In this context the following review of Loren's early comedy Too Bad She's Bad offers some interesting pointers:

> The dialogue appears to be full of lively gags, but for the audience, there is certainly more reading than looking. When Sophia Loren is on the screen it becomes completely maddening. Our advice to all non-Italian speakers is: forget the story, forget the subtitles, just watch the dame. (Crowther: 1955)

For a non-native speaker the problem of understanding 'lively gags' in another language raises more general questions about the exportability of certain genre forms. Comedy is heavily dependent on grasping fully the subtleties of meaning of the spoken word and, as a result, it is perhaps the genre form least successful in making the transition from one culture to another. The international success for European action-adventures, horror films, and Spaghetti Westerns may, on the other hand, be attributable to the predominantly visual emphasis of their content (Hudson 2006: 22). Furthermore, failing to grasp the meaning of the words is only part of the effort of understanding the whole comic performance on the screen. Referring to popular French cinema,

Jeancolas uses the term 'inexportable' in relation to certain types of films that are 'destined to be seen only by spectators in their country of origin [and] unintelligible to spectators outside a given cultural area' (Jeancolas 1992: 141). Quick repartee, gestures and body language are inextricably linked and are integral to the performance in the comedy films that were essential to establishing Loren's early screen persona. It is thus not difficult to see the problems for her of transferring to a different film culture that, in any case, had its own established comic conventions. In the face of the struggles of the US industry on the 1950s, Guback famously quotes a distributor as advising his counterparts in the exhibition sector to 'consider ways and means of popularizing the foreign film', and 'establish an audience where there had been none before' (Guback 1976: 399). This scenario of course generated a market for the arthouse productions of Fellini and De Sica. The innovative qualities of European arthouse production found a receptive US market, but the heyday was short-lived, as Hollywood production companies and film-makers quickly adapted to a changed postwar market (Balio 1998: 63).

For Loren's forte, romantic comedy, the prospects for success were much less promising. The United States had its own vibrant comic tradition from the 1930s romantic comedies of Ernst Lubitsch, to the screwball comedies that showcased the skills of Cary Grant and assorted partners. At the time of Loren's transfer to Hollywood the comic genre had received fresh impetus with the work of Doris Day. Day came to the fore in films such as *The Pajama Game* (Donen and Abbott, 1957) and went on to forge a highly successful comic partnership with Rock Hudson in *Pillow Talk* (Gordon, 1959), and *Lover Come Back* (Delbert Mann, 1961) where her on-screen persona as the independent 'bachelor girl' resonated in ways that were specific to US culture. However, when Loren arrived in Hollywood, the industry put a price on her that suggested they prized her prospects more highly than those of her American counterparts. This triggered a *Photoplay* enquiry fronted by a large photo of Loren and a lengthy article appropriately entitled, 'What's she got that Hollywood hasn't?' (Sheppard 1957: 33): it focused on the recent Hollywood tendency to buy in European talent, and emphasized the growing tendency in Hollywood to recognize stars of European origin, particularly marked in recent Academy Awards for best actress, to Audrey Hepburn (1954) for *Roman Holiday*, Anna Magnani for *The Rose Tattoo* (Daniel Mann, 1955), and Ingrid Bergman for *Anastasia* (Litvak, 1956). But in terminology drawn from the same magazine we also find a possible source of obstacles to Loren's success. The *Photoplay* edition of 12 December 1957 set up its annual invitation for readers to vote for their favourite stars, and listed Loren among the possible candidates in the category of 'Best Newcomer of 1957' as 'the new Italian pin-up'. Opinion polls and awards are clearly not fully reliable, being based on notions of 'popular appeal' and 'critical acclaim' that themselves have only the vaguest of definitions. But two polls of the period offer some degree of understanding of Loren's place in the US market. Although proposed by the magazine as a possible contender for *Photoplay*'s 'Best Newcomer of 1957' Loren receives no mention at all in the poll results, reported in the edition of 16 March 1958, and assembled from the votes of the magazine's readers. This result contrasts sharply with an annual US industry poll entitled 'Stars of Tomorrow' carried out by the trade magazine *Motion Picture Herald*. Each year distributors and exhibitors of the industry voted for the stars they judged to have the greatest box-office potential in the year ahead. In their 1957 poll, they placed Loren second behind Anthony Perkins, her co-star in *Desire under the Elms*. Paramount counted the result of sufficient significance as a promotional tool as to take out a full-page advert in the said *Motion Picture Herald* on 19 October 1957 that read 'Paramount proudly presents the actors voted the top two "Stars of Tomorrow" in *Desire under the Elms,* the latest Paramount picture and a film that is powerfully dramatic and frank'. As we shall see, the film performed poorly at the box-office and it becomes evident that by 1957 the era of the pin-up – so closely associated with the posters GIs pinned on their lockers in wartime – was fast dissipating. US stars Rita Hayworth and Jane Russell had left this phase of their careers behind, and another Hollywood diva Ava Gardner, was by then largely Europe-based.

The rapidly-shifting nature of late 1950s film-making perhaps explains the fact that in the case of Loren perceptions of those managing the Hollywood industry were not entirely in tune with the preferences of their audiences. Other emerging female stars of the era presented a physicality that bore little resemblance to earlier American pin-ups, and their male co-stars also demonstrated a changing Hollywood agenda. One can cite numerous examples of relevant films and the new breed of US stars, many of whom were closely associated with the method-acting techniques of the Actors' Studio: Kim Novak's work in *Man with the Golden Arm* (Preminger, 1955; co-star: Frank Sinatra) and *Vertigo* (Hitchcock, 1958; co-star: James Stewart); Lee Remick in *Anatomy of a Murder* (Preminger, 1959; co-star: Ben Gazzara) and *River Wild* (Kazan, 1960; co-star: Montgomery Clift), and Eva Marie Saint in *On the Waterfront* (Kazan 1954; co star: Marlon Brando). In the case of Brando and Dean the films' focus becomes the body of the male star, articulating a form of sexuality very different from films of the studio era. In summary, this was an emerging form of film-making where Loren quite simply appeared ill-placed.[12] As a 'pin-up' she gave continuity to traditional star images that associated her with a fast-fading era of 'old' Hollywood. We shall now consider how these elements were presented in the individual films, to assess the degree of Loren's success in Hollywood.

The Loren persona: Modifications and transformations

As we saw, the films of the Hollywood years may easily be subdivided in accordance with production arrangements; in turn these phases contribute very different facets to the evolution of the Loren persona. Whether shot in Europe or in Hollywood, all the productions of this period share certain characteristics that underline the industry's willingness to invest in Loren. They feature high-level co-stars, experienced directors (Kramer, Curtiz, Cukor), the expertise of leading technical exponents (Jack Cardiff as director of photography in *Legend of the Lost*, Paramount's head of costume Edith Head) and high production values evidenced in set and costume design, and the extensive periods of location shooting. However, within the individual groupings, there are marked differences to the persona constructed by Loren's roles. In the three runaway productions filmed before she moved to the US, Loren is teamed with ageing stars of traditional Hollywood. As Molly Haskell notes (1987: 16) it was perfectly normal for male screen stars to go on playing romantic leads from one generation to another, while their early (female) partners 'go wilting into retirement'. We thus have the spectacle in all three films of a 23-year-old Loren teamed with leading men Cary Grant (aged 54) John Wayne (aged 50), and the youngest, the 44-year-old Alan Ladd. Within Italian national cinema Loren's roles were expressive of a popular culture projected through the tradition of national film comedy. As Chapters 4 and 5 will show, her performance in these early comedies with De Sica and

Mastroianni is finely judged and characterized by verbal and body language at once extravagant and subtly played out. In the runaway productions all such nuances are discarded. The nature of her performance in the various roles, whether located in the Libyan desert (*Legend of the Lost*) or on the Spanish plain (*The Pride and the Passion*), is exaggerated and declamatory. In contrast to the verbal sparring of the Italian comedies she says little. What she does convey is found in her dress, facial expression and stance, where she takes on associations of transgression associated with the gypsy or Oriental woman; this largely re-consigned her to the one-dimensional delineation typical of her photo-romance roles. Whether her character is identified notionally as Spanish, Greek or North African there is a distinct blurring of identities into a stereotypical, vaguely pan-Mediterranean role (Gundle 1995: 372). In consequence her performance presents itself as reduced to a range of striking pin-up poses: the 'sexy shots' of her mentioned by *Variety* must surely have included stills from *Boy on a Dolphin* as she emerges from the sea, the wet, skimpy clothes highlighting her curvaceous body. The practice persisted in later films, and it is notable that the shots most often repeated (in stills, posters and DVD covers) are of a scantily-clad Loren in *The Millionairess* as Epifania Parerga, where she undresses for a supposed medical examination by the Peter Sellers' figure Doctor Kabir, and as Mara the prostitute who does a striptease for the trainee priest, played by Marcello Mastroianni in Episode 2 of *Yesterday, Today and Tomorrow*.

Once in Hollywood, the strategy changes again, and here the films are exceptionally unadventurous in the use they make (or more accurately do not make) of the sexual charge of Loren's screen potential. The subject-matter of her first film, *Desire under the Elms* suggests otherwise: she is an Italian immigrant who, desperate for assimilation into US society, marries an ageing Southern farmer and embarks on an incestuous relationship with his son. However, the finished film lacks the powerful, subversive potential of the original script. As all film-making is a collaborative undertaking we cannot attribute the film's lack of success to a single individual. But we may usefully compare the fortunes of *Desire under the Elms* to those of a very similar production from the following year, *Cat on a Hot Tin Roof* (Marshall, 1958). The two films shared a script originating in theatre (by, respectively, Eugene O'Neill and Tennessee Williams), location (a sultry, claustrophobic South), plot (generational father-against-son conflict) and shared casting (in both films Burl Ives plays the domineering father). Yet the work of Loren and rising star Anthony Perkins received nothing similar to the accolades (Academy Award nominations, rapturous critical reviews, box-office success) for the performances of Liz Taylor and Paul Newman in the later film. Of the films produced in the early Hollywood years, only two, *The Pride and the Passion* and *Houseboat* are listed by *Motion Picture Herald* as achieving high box-office returns. The other major success, *Two Women* was produced in 1960, and not by Paramount; by this time Loren's main Paramount contract had run out and she had returned to Europe.[13] Since the Kramer film had also incurred ruinously high location costs, the director himself classed the film as 'a bomb' (Spoto 1978: 187). This leaves the only real success of the Hollywood years as *Houseboat*, a film that gave Loren some scope to express her comic skills. It also teamed her with Cary Grant, one of the great exponents of the American comic tradition where, as part of a successful formula, he is coupled with elegant international co-stars – Grace Kelly in *To Catch a Thief* (Hitchcock, 1955) and Audrey Hepburn in *Charade* (Donen, 1963). Notably in the same period it is again through the medium of comedy that Loren achieves another international success, *The Millionairess* (Asquith, 1960) with co-star Peter Sellers.

Despite extensive costs and efforts on the part of the film-makers, the remaining roles had very indifferent commercial and critical fortunes. As we have noted, a change of contract took place when Loren returned to Hollywood from filming *The Key* in England. Given the success of Ponti's ventures within the ambit of Italian film-making, his joint production role with Marcello Girosi, who had contributed to the production of several Loren films earlier in the decade, did not salvage the progress of Loren's Hollywood film career artistically or commercially. It would be mistaken, however, to believe that, as a media personality, Loren was in any sense *un*popular with the American public. Within the new medium of television, she made prestigious appearances in shows such as the Ed Murrow weekly interview programme, and a highly paid spot on the Perry Como show that was widely reported in the American and Italian press. Nevertheless, in the latter stages of her several Hollywood contracts, her cinematic career took the form of a gradual 'withdrawal' to Europe in relation to: location (shooting of the last two films), production supervision (the effective shift from Paramount's to Ponti and Girosi's control), casting (John Gavin was the only non-European lead in *A Breath of Scandal*), and perhaps most significantly, of funding. With *A Breath of Scandal* there was a return to the system of *compartecipazione*: it was an Italo-American co-production between Titanus and Paramount, supported by the usual subsidies from the Italian government, a pattern of funding that suggested Paramount had increasingly less confidence in Loren's earning potential as a star. The concluding film of the Paramount era *It Started in Naples* has the semblance of a final attempt to present Loren as a Hollywood product. It featured a script that brought out the worst possible national stereotypes, both Italian and American. It combined Loren, an empty-headed Southern local with a heart and an ageing Clark Gable, a former GI bringing anti-Italian prejudices (and toothpaste) to the country, as he searches for the son conceived during his wartime stay. The film is marked by a creakingly explicit strategy to assemble what were clearly perceived as the standard ingredients for commercial success of a Loren runaway production: setting (picture-postcard Capri), a sexy dance (echoes of the dance sequence in the castle courtyard in *The Pride and the Passion*, and even the earlier *The Woman of the River*), and a range of subsidiary characters, including Vittorio De Sica, acting out a scenario of hackneyed local roles that bore not the slightest resemblance to the lives of contemporary Italians in the early 1960s. The film effectively closed the Hollywood years, a period that latterly took on the semblance of a career spiralling downwards, what *Life* suggested 'seemed like the beginning of a lingering end for Loren' (Hamblin 1961: 25). A star's image, however, is forged not only by his/her films: publicity and promotion also play an important role, and the case study will now consider the significance of these elements in relation to Loren's career.

Case study: Sophia Loren – reading the pictures

Sophia Loren's 'life in pictures' merits a study in itself and indeed a collection of shots has been published recently with this very title (Verlhac and Dherbier 2008). However, shots of Loren have importance over and above their potential as pages in picture-books. Her career is marked by a close affinity to the camera, with many examples of cleverly staged press-shots used as a publicity tool. A number of publications listed in the bibliography give evidence of her extended collaborations with eminent photographers Tazio Secchiaroli, Richard Avedon, Pierluigi Praturlon and Alfred Eisenstadt that came about slightly later in her career, from the 1960s onwards. For the sake of brevity the case study is limited to reading three earlier shots that give valuable insight into the function played by the still photo in developing her career. The part played in constructing Loren's image by other media forms, in particular the photo-romances and the cine-romances was analysed in Chapter 2: the chapter noted also the widespread diffusion of her image on magazine covers in Europe and in the United States, the so-called 'ephemera' that made her face familiar to a wide-ranging public, some of whom had never bought a ticket to see a Loren film. To a degree all star images draw on this extra-textual material, but it was a dimension particularly significant to the careers of a range of shapely stars of Loren's time, from Marilyn Monroe to Diana Dors, Anita Ekberg, Gina Lollobrigida and Jayne Mansfield.

Figure 2: Sophia, Yvonne de Carlo and Gina Lollobrigida at the Berlin Film Festival June 1954. Kobal Collection.

Figure 2 is a shot of Sophia Loren, Gina Lollobrigida and Yvonne De Carlo at the fourth Berlin Film Festival of June 1954. The two Italian stars had films in competition at the event, respectively *Neapolitan Carousel* and *Bread, Love and Dreams*. The Festival's major prize, the Golden Bear for Best Film, was awarded by the popular vote of festival delegates. In 1954 the winner was the British film *Hobson's Choice*, directed by David Lean, with Lollobrigida's *Bread, Love and Dreams* achieving a very creditable second place. The shot was taken at the Festival's closing event on 29 June, and several versions were published in the national and international press at the time. It is essential to note that it is a shot that predates the emergence of Loren as a major star. When *The Gold of Naples* premiered in Rome in December 1954 it set up a convenient framework to this particular 'battle of the busts': their rivalry was from this time forward couched in terms of a struggle for popularity between the newly emerging *la pizzaiola* (Loren's role in the De Sica film), and *la bersagliera*, Lollobrigida's already very successful part in the first two films of the series. However, this is an earlier shot that shows little evidence of a rivalry between them. On the contrary, they appear satisfied in each other's company, happy to take the opportunity for a shared publicity pose. It is a scenario that was without doubt to Loren's considerable advantage because it positions them as stars of apparently equal importance, sharing the aura of their equally important status. The detail of their careers at this time shows this to be an impression that is mistaken, and almost entirely false.

Here, in every sense, Lollobrigida was the major star, her film being one of the great successes of the current festival. By mid-1954 *Bread, Love and Dreams* had already achieved great success for the production company, Gustavo Lombardo's Titanus films, and was the top-grossing film of the 1953–4 national film season. Lollobrigida was also a star well-known internationally and who, despite a truncated Hollywood career, had now fully re-established her leading European status. Loren, on the other hand, had scarcely emerged in a major screen role. *Neapolitan Carousel*, her film entered in competition, was, like the later *The Gold of Naples*, an 'episode film' that showcased a collective cast rather than an individual star role. The shot is also part of a wide range of photographic and written evidence showing that both actresses were keenly aware of the advantages of following the festival circuit to enhance their careers. At the Cannes Film Festival in the 1950s and early 1960s, alongside a range of important directors and other actors, Loren and Lollobrigida were major exponents of Italy's new-found glamour in the cinema world and beyond (Corless and Darke 2007: 78). At such events the advantage was clearly reciprocal: shots like this benefited both the career of the stars, and in turn the image of the festival itself. However, information from the official Festival report published by the Berlin Press Bureau gives this argument an important additional dimension. The report states that Loren and Lollobrigida were part of the official delegation sent to represent Italy at the event. The other members were Under-Secretary of State Giuseppe Ermini and a senior administrator Annnibale Scicluna, both from the Ministry of Entertainment and Tourism; Renato Gualino, in his capacity as president of the International Association of Film Producers; and a prominent film director of the time, Augusto Genina. In this small, representative grouping the surprise is surely the inclusion of Loren, an actress whose film career had scarcely begun. Were there not other more prominent, successful stars better suited to representing Italian cinema in 1954? Perhaps in the light of photo-opportunities such as this, the answer is negative. Loren's highly photogenic qualities, coupled with those of Lollobrigida, contribute to an occasion that becomes not just a casual publicity opportunity for the two stars, but part of a more concerted promotional strategy devised by the Italian film industry. The meaning we have read in the shot – that Loren is equal in status to Lollobrigida – is reinforced by her selection, itself debatable, as one of the two actress delegates representing Italy. Once the premiere of The Gold of Naples took place in December 1954 reports of a strong rivalry between the two stars gathered pace. To what extent this was generated by the stars themselves, and to what extent it emanated from the press is not clear.[14] Either way, as we saw in the Chapter 2, to avoid continued comparisons, Loren and Lollobrigida increasingly avoided meeting at public events such as this. As a consequence it is an example of a joint shot that was to become very rare indeed.

The presence of De Carlo gives a further interesting dimension to this discussion. She offers the spectacle of a personality pushing in on a show already established – the Loren–Lollobrigida show. This puts her in a position of inferiority since it appears that it is she who is trying to gain advantage from their presence. Again, the impression conveyed by the shot does not match the facts. De Carlo was a well-regarded US actress with a range of central starring roles in films of the 1940s. As the festival report records, she was welcomed with great enthusiasm at the event; however it was also noted that the actress was present at the instigation of (unnamed) European producers with whom she was working at the time. Like a number of major stars of the studio era such as Gregory Peck and William Holden, De Carlo was now supplementing her Hollywood work with contracts in the increasingly lucrative European market, a market where she was obliged to compete with stars with a national-popular appeal. While her position in Hollywood had been assured, the experience of stars in the post-studio market was, as we have noted, much less stable. For De Carlo then, the image carries a meaning specific to the detail of her contemporary career in that she is the figure new to the context of European film-making. But she can also be seen as a representative presence conveying aspects of the relationship of US–European stars at this time. Surveying Loren's career potential in Hollywood, we noted the significance of the article entitled 'What's she got that Hollywood hasn't?' We might amend this to give this shot the caption, 'What have they [Loren and Lollobrigda] got that she [De Carlo] hasn't?' The question can be posed not as a reflection of the competence of the individual actresses concerned but simply to acknowledge that for the briefest of periods Loren and Lollobrigida gained the ascendancy over their Hollywood rivals.

Figure 3 shows Loren, Louella Parsons and Jayne Mansfield at one of the welcoming parties arranged to mark her arrival in Hollywood. The event took place in Los Angeles at Romanoff's night club, shortly after Loren's arrival in early April, and on 6 May Life devoted six pages to reporting it. Despite the casual air – a moment created spontaneously at a celebrity event – we know this to be part of a carefully orchestrated campaign to launch Loren. The three US majors that had just produced her films ensured that many of their own photographers were present, and a range of shots of the event quickly went into circulation.[15] Superficially, the shot bears comparison with the one taken at the Berlin Festival. The seated figures carry the authority of the shot while the standing figure, bending over, appears as an intruder pushing in on the main players. At this point Mansfield was the better-known personality, having worked for several years in Hollywood; her appearance here was clearly understood as a publicity stunt for her forthcoming film Will Success Spoil Rock Hudson? (Tashlin, 1957). Mansfield was renowned for just this kind of move to make the headlines,

Figure 3: Sophia, Jayne Mansfield and Louella Parsons at Romanoff's April 1957. Kobal Collection.

and this is one of many similar shots that characterized her career. Despite her efforts, we can say that in fact the stance of Mansfield serves to enhance Loren's presence in a manner that considerably favours the Italian star. The shot presents a seated Loren who, although barely off the plane from Italy, already has the appearance of an established star graciously acknowledging an opportunistic new arrival. The presence of Parsons gives further complexity to the shot. Parsons had been the doyenne of the Hollywood gossip world and, for a time, her approval and support for a star in her newspaper column was a great fillip to the progress of a star career. By 1957 this was no longer the case. A changing Hollywood scenario left Parsons associated with the studio era: her capacity to assess the qualities of the newer rising stars such as Dean and Brando was less assured, and in general her authority as a keen observer of the Hollywood scene was in decline (Kashner and MacNair 2002: 280). The fact that she was present at the function is testimony to her long-established status on the Hollywood scene, but the effect is double-edged. On the one hand it was surely intended as a compliment, designed to contribute positively to Loren's Hollywood debut; on the other hand we may see the effect as negative as it continues the tendency of implicitly associating Loren's persona with Hollywood's past, associations that meant she was to fit awkwardly or not at all into a cinematic context in a state of considerable flux. *Photoplay* welcomed the actress with the headline '*Benvenuto* (sic) Sophia' with similar shots of the event, but as this analysis shows, they relay to the viewer, if not to Loren, a very mixed message as to what lay ahead for her in Hollywood (Wilkes 1957: 18).

'Outlawed for Love'

The stated aim of this chapter was to identify 'the ways in which [Loren's] evolving persona was presented in Italy and internationally, on screen and in the press'. So far the chapter has noted the very marked contrasts in the raw materials (films and even magazine spreads) by which Italian, as against US, audiences accessed the star, and between tentative career beginnings in Italy, and the substantial studio promotion that accompanied Loren's Hollywood debut. But contrasting perceptions are also strongly apparent in relation to Loren's personal circumstances, that is, in the response to complications surrounding her marriage to Carlo Ponti. At a time when the press and the public had little enthusiasm for her films, a series of events sustained her profile in other ways. Rather than a single shot, this section highlights repeated press images of Loren and Ponti at various airports across the world. One of these, on page 5 of the magazine *Vie nuove* issued on 10 January 1959 is accompanied by the above caption 'outlawed for love' (*I fuorilegge dell'amore*), typical of the colourful press headlines the couple had to endure at this time. The shot is of a weary Loren and Ponti at an unnamed airport, caught seemingly unawares as they hurry from the plane. Though hardly in itself a publicity stunt, photos of this type maintained for Loren a high level of exposure, relentless public attention that at the time was not otherwise evident in the reception of her films. The difficulties of Loren's personal life are given the fullest possible coverage in her numerous biographies. They will be summarized, in order to lead on to the very interesting question of how they impacted on her star image. Shortly after she arrived in the United States, Ponti obtained a divorce under Mexican law from his first wife, and he and Loren were married by proxy, again under Mexican law, in September 1957. However, the legality of this marriage was challenged in the Italian courts and, since the courts did not recognize divorce, charges of bigamy were laid against Ponti. While the case was under consideration in Italy, it was inadvisable for him and Loren to spend protracted periods of time on Italian soil, in case of arrest. By late 1958 it was not clear whether Loren would continue to work in Hollywood: at the same time, it was clear that a definitive relocation to Italy was decidedly ill-advised. What then followed was a period when her life took the form of semi-exile from her native country, a way of living described in *Italia domani* of 11 January 1959 as 'a wandering existence, moving from one departure lounge to another, from one elegant home to another'. Ponti and Loren took up residence in Paris. As a result of long involvement in Franco–Italian film productions, Ponti had extensive business interests in the French capital, where, in addition to the Rome base, his Champion production company had its other main outlet. The couple applied for French nationality, and this eventually enabled them to obtain a divorce and marry in 1966.

The vilification of Loren that followed the bigamy charges provided colourful press reporting: this included the intervention of the Vatican that threatened excommunication to 'those who transgress against moral and religious law' (Moscati 2005: 156–7). But this tone of condemnation was certainly not uniform, and commentary even from within Italy itself was by no means entirely hostile. There is much evidence of support for Loren, across a range of sources. Firstly, she continued to receive substantial recognition in her professional life: in September 1958 she was awarded the Coppa Volpi for best actress at the Venice Film Festival for the film *The Black Orchid*, and again as best actress for the same film in 1959 voted by Italian press critics at the national Donatello awards. At the time, international commentators registered astonishment at the Venice result. *The Black Orchid* is surely one of the actress's least meritorious films; however, at the very least, the awards demonstrate a continuing level of popularity for Loren within Italy. It is also conceivable that they were allocated as a gesture of opposition to the harshly critical standpoint adopted by conservative forces in Italy. The popular press was absolutely explicit in its support: on 11 January 1959 *Italia domani* announced its intention to 'defend Sofia Loren against those casting the stone of scandal against her'. The magazine went on to speak of the 'hypocrisy' of reports on the 1958 Venice Film Festival that on the one hand openly recorded criticism of Loren, while on the other hand enthusiastically displaying provocative shots of two other visitors to the event, Anita Ekberg and Brigitte Bardot. The short report accompanying the *Vie nuove* picture also used the term 'hypocrisy' in its criticism of the treatment of 'our much-loved actress'. Press interest intensified when Loren's arrival to film in Italy became imminent. She worked first in Vienna filming *A Breath of Scandal*, and completed the film at Cinecittà, then transferred to Capri to begin shooting *It Happened in Naples* with Clark Gable. The positive tenor of attendant reports is unmistakable, with headlines such as 'Back in Italy at last' in *Noi donne* (8 August 1959) and 'Italy holds its breath as Sophia returns' (Marotta 1959: 16). In a four-page spread with accompanying shots of Loren in transit, *Oggi* reported that Loren was making the journey from Vienna to Rome, 'with her heart in her mouth, full of the emotion felt at returning to her native land' (Sansa 1959: 10). Responsibility for the charge of 'hypocrisy' was left suitably vague, but without doubt Loren's experience triggered debate on questions of public opinion and personal morality, that took the form of a kind of open, national self-questioning. This was surely new, and indicative of a shift from the Catholic conservatism of the immediate postwar to the beginnings of a less hidebound perspective of the society emerging from Italy's economic boom.

The tenor of international reports gives an equally interesting picture of changes wrought in the decade of the 1950s. Initially we find in the *Photoplay* of 5 October 1957 a cheerful, non-judgmental headline, 'Sophia's gone and done it!' For the American press this was only one of many tales of divorce and remarriage that occupied their pages. Unsurprisingly, in the same period the saga of Elizabeth Taylor's many marriages and divorces eclipsed the more simple Loren saga. Once the supposed scandal broke, a pattern emerges where the emphasis is on detaching American press and American public opinion from the extremes of reaction in Italy. *Photoplay* reported the 'blast' of criticism from the Vatican, balancing this against its own portrait of the couple and 'the quiet life they share, the hours spent away from the glamour whirl, cozily sharing a plate of warmed-up spaghetti' (Lewis 1958: 69). A major overview of Loren's career in *Life*, dated August 1961, when the Hollywood years were already concluded, reported that the Italian authorities have 'slapped [Loren and Ponti] with a bigamy charge', a form of public condemnation set against the writer's own description of the couple as 'models of marital content' (Hamblin 1961: 28). It is essential to note how sharply these reports contrast with the treatment meted out to two major stars little less than ten years before. In 1949 the case of Ingrid Bergman and her liaison with Roberto Rossellini elicited condemnation from American press and politicians alike (Damico 1991: 8). In Italy, it is suggested, the attitude of the press was 'quite circumspect', with the voice of the Church less prominent in attacks on the star (Gundle 2000: 73). Nevertheless on both sides of the Atlantic there was unanimity in the use of the term 'scandal' to label Bergman's conduct. The case of Ava Gardner also dates from the period 1949 to 1950. Though less high-profile and largely restricted to the American context where her career was located, it had many parallels with Bergman's. Gardner's relationship with Frank Sinatra, at the time struggling to establish his career, made her – and only her – the object of the public's antipathy. Sinatra was married and the scandal intensified in February 1950 when Nancy Sinatra made a statement to the press about her marriage. In the resulting burst of negative publicity, Gardner received many letters from the public, some addressing her as 'dear bitch', and identifying her as 'the snake' supposedly responsible for breaking up a solid Catholic marriage (Server 2006: 184–5).

The perspective taken in the *Life* report on Loren demonstrates how decidedly public opinion had shifted in the course of a decade. To a degree all publicity is welcome, and accounts of the troubled life of a glamorous star continue to boost press sales to this day. However, the reporting on Loren, Bergman and Gardner retains our interest for a number or reasons. Throughout, there is the assumption that responsibility for a relationship with a married man largely belonged to the female partner. The notion of the 'scarlet woman' persisted, while much less effort was devoted to reflections on the conduct of Rossellini, Sinatra or Ponti: but ten years on from Bergman and Gardner, judgment on Loren was no longer unanimous. Instead, the widest possible range of views is apparent, from hardened critical to more open-minded liberal. Some questions, inevitably speculative, remain. To what extent did the diversified audience of Loren in the late 1950s defuse the drama of her 'scandal'? How damaging would these events have been to Loren's career if her persona had been restricted to the national arena? Debates and disagreements were aired in the press and this in itself kept Loren's persona strongly in focus despite her faltering on-screen fortunes. The caption 'outlawed for love' summarizes well the intersecting of a number of aspects relevant to the question. It suggests a certain frisson in the thrill of the chase (of reporters trying to catch a shot of the wandering couple) as well as a sense of the illicit, labelling their relationship in a way that, conversely, the accompanying text sets about challenging vigorously. The caption is in fact intensely sympathetic to the couple, openly showing support for them and critical of the cumbersome and outdated legal system that effectively banned them from setting foot on Italian soil. We shall see that, partly as a result of this widespread support, Loren did not encounter the commercial ostracism that Hollywood exerted in the case of Ingrid Bergman. The next chapter will show that on her definitive return to Europe there were considerable reserves of popularity and financial backing that proved more than sufficient to launch a new, more successful phase of Sophia Loren's career.

Notes

1. In the drive to influence the rebuilding of Europe, the Americans were well aware of the importance of film in establishing cultural hegemony; consequently in the immediate postwar period film matters handled by the Allies were dealt with by a section of the PWB (Psychological War Bureau). For a comprehensive study of America's continued involvement in the politics of postwar Italy see David Ellwood's *Rebuilding Europe: Western Europe, America and Postwar Reconstruction*, in particular pp. 114–17. As Ellwood shows, America played a decisive role in the success of the Christian Democrats in 1948, mounting the first example of a 'major counter offensive' to ensure defeat for the Left (Ellwood 1999: 115).

2. In all, Loren featured on seven *Life* covers that included six solo appearances: 22 August 1955, 6 May 1957, 14 November 1960, 11 August 1961, 18 September 1964, 16 September 1966, and one with Charlie Chaplin on 1 April 1966. It is a most remarkable tally that in itself is a means of measuring her international success. Comparative figures for cover appearances of other Italian stars are Lollobrigida (2), Mangano (1) and Elsa Martinelli (1). A more useful point of comparison is probably cover shots of Monroe (8) and of Liz Taylor (9).

3. The producers' views, that were not surprisingly largely positive, are found in a number of interviews published in *Cinema nuovo*, edited by Braccio Agnoletti (1956: 135–37). The opinions of local workers are rather different, as shown in correspondence in individual archive files. For example, there were extended discussions between William Wyler, the director of *Roman Holiday* and union representatives to ensure employment for Italian rather than American technicians on the film (ACS/MV/*Roman Holiday*).

4. Bernardini (1982: 234) classifies Italian funding of *The Legend of the Lost* in the category of 'minority status (*minoritario italiano*)', meaning that the other listed contributor (here, the United States) made the majority contribution. Correspondence in the film's archive file shows that at first the application for state support was strongly opposed. An unidentified official wrote an initial report recommending that approval be refused. The report asked, 'is it really in the interests of the Italian film industry to support this film with Sophia Loren? Surely her presence favours the interest of the film's American producer, and not ours? Why should we support a practice that effectively facilitates the efforts of non-Italian filmmakers to rob our industry of its most prominent, money-making stars?' (ACS/MV/*Legend of the Lost*). Approval was nevertheless forthcoming, but emerged again in a similar but much more public controversy that surrounded the funding of Loren's later film with Charlton Heston, *El Cid* (Anthony Mann, 1962) details of which will be discussed in Chapter 5.

5. Quaglietti offers a fascinating account of the meeting. The Board was headed by Admiral Stone, and Quaglietti identifies the other members as follows: US Army Captain Pilade Levi; Stephen Pallos, ex-assistant to Alexander Korda, representing the British Army; Alfredo Guarini representing the personnel of the Italian film industry; and Alfredo Proia, representing the industry's financiers. Stone opened the meeting stating that 'the Italian cinema has to be wiped out', which he later clarified as meaning that he considered it necessary to destroy the way Fascism had organized the industry (Quaglietti 1974: 5). Guarini himself gives a partial account of the same meeting in 'Il neorealismo e l'industria', *Cinema* 123 (15 December 1953) 75–77.

6. The details of Levi's career at Paramount Film, Italy are difficult to trace, but he is still active and cited in correspondence as being closely involved in Paramount budget negotiations in 1960 to fund filming of *It Started in Naples* (ACS/PF/*It Started in Naples*).

7. De Laurentiis continued his productions in Italy, funding for a time the development of activities at a set of studios dubbed *Dinocittà*. Following the failure of this venture he eventually transferred to the United States, where he oversaw a number of very successful productions. His career and personal life is fully documented in Kezich and Levantesi (2001).

8. Lollobrigida's was quite literally 'the face of Italian cinema' on the cover of *Time*, dated 16 August 1954, containing an extensive (ten-page) and much-quoted article entitled 'Hollywood by the Tiber'. It analyses the phenomenon of the inter-relationship between Italian and American film industries from a US perspective with the personality of Lollobrigida as a key reference point.

9. For accounts by Italian actors of their experience in Hollywood see the section with an intentionally ironic title, 'Hollywood Romance' in Faldini and Fofi (1979: 311–13). There are contributions, some very bitter, from Rossano Brazzi, Valentina Cortese, Alida Valli, and the book's editor, Franca Faldini. Both Valli and Cortese worked under studio contract, and recount their difficulties in adjusting to the demands of the studio system. Anna Magnani achieved Oscar success in the US production *The Rose Tattoo* (Daniel Mann, 1954) but returned to Italy, unconvinced that she belonged within the trappings of Hollywood. The short-lived Hollywood careers of Mastroianni and Vittorio Gassman are briefly summarized in the glossary section of Philips and Vincendeau (2006). To this list we might add the name of Pier Angeli whose Hollywood career included a highly successful role alongside Paul Newman in *Someone Up There Likes Me* (1956), but thereafter had only intermittent screen success. The press linked her romantically to James Dean, and she went on to marry Vic Damone, the Italo-American singer, and later Armando Trovaioli, composer of Italian film music. Both marriages ended in divorce, and she died of a drug overdose in 1962 at the age of 39. On the other hand Angeli's sister Marisa Pavan was cast with Magnani in *The Rose Tattoo* for which role she won an Oscar as best supporting actress.

10. For a summary of contract issues in the period 1945–1960, see the chapter 'The rise of labour unions', in Gomery (2005), *The Hollywood System*, pp. 185–97. He notes the 1945 De Havilland decision which declared that 'the studios could no longer contract players for more than seven years' but records that, by 1950, 'nearly all stars had hired their own agent' and 'the studios were happy to no longer have seven-year-contract commitments' (p. 195), though the cited cases of Lollobrigida and Monroe make clear that this was only partially true.

11. The list has been compiled from information detailed in the cited publications, the trade journals of the US industry. The journals present an annual listing of all films granted screening rights in the relevant year, and record the date of the first screening of the film in the United States. Two of Loren's 1950s films had later release dates: *Attila* (1954) through Joseph Levine's Embassy Pictures in 1958, and the very early *A Day in Court* (1952) in 1962. Levine's role in distributing and marketing Loren's films of the 1960s will be extensively discussed in Chapters 4 and 5.

12. Much later, Loren and Brando did co-star in *The Countess from Hong Kong* (Chaplin, 1967), but by then the significance of the persona of both stars was substantially altered.

13. For further information on the source of US box-office figures, see 'Note to sources and references' in the bibliography.

14. For further comment on this event see Rondi's chapter on Loren (1998: 296–305). It is his opinion that neither actress was particularly hostile to the other, and that the story of their rivalry was from its inception a publicity strategy.

15. It is clear that the publicity machine for Loren was set in motion at the earliest opportunity. As we saw earlier in the chapter, it was there in the press shots of her even before she left Italian soil. An extended

report on subsequent events is found in *Life* on 6 May 1957 has the heading 'Roman Holiday in Hollywood', and is a useful source of details about these events. The report states that Paramount, for whom she was about to work, handled the official welcome at Los Angeles airport, where a press conference with 'more than 100' studio executives, agents and reporters was held. Twentieth Century Fox, producers of *Boy on a Dolphin* organized the party at Romanoff's from which this shot is taken. To promote *The Pride and the Passion*, premiered in July, Stanley Kramer held a similar event attended by 500 guests with stars Loren and Cary Grant present, 'an event so big that it had to be held on a studio sound stage'.

4

LOREN AND DE SICA

Sophia goes to the movies

On 3 April 1953 the photo-romance *Sogno* dedicated its cover to a photo and a lengthy caption that read, 'this unforgettable interpreter of so many of our photo-romances has been taken away from us by the world of cinema. But Sofia has not forgotten her readers, male and female, and it is to them that she dedicates this, her final souvenir and farewell'. As the era of Sofia Lazzaro the photo-romance cover-girl concluded, so her film career as Sophia Loren gathered pace. Table 1 on the next page shows that in the period 1952–5 she appeared on Italian cinema screens with remarkable regularity.[1]

Critics, as well as Loren herself, have attributed her screen success to the guidance of Vittorio De Sica, and the detail of their collaboration, tied to two distinct chronological periods, will be examined in this chapter. The early period was followed by the Hollywood years. Their partnership resumed again with the filming of *Two Women* in 1960, followed by a return to comedy in the immediate aftermath of that film's success. This same chronology is largely replicated in Loren's partnership with Marcello Mastroianni. The task of subdividing these elements is therefore to a degree artificial. Even though Loren's involvement with De Sica overlaps with her film-making with Mastroianni, the separate strands of these collaborations deserve further consideration. The particular focus here will be on evidence from the Central State Archive that modifies substantially the received understanding of the separate roles of Loren and De Sica, and the dynamic of their collaboration in Italian cinema history.

As in the chapter on Ponti, it is important here to base analysis of a professional relationship neither solely on an individual personality, nor on an individual pairing, in isolation. The suggestion that Loren was 'discovered' or 'launched' by De Sica is too simplistic. Rather, her career in comedy, the mainstay of this early phase, drew on a very wide range of artistic skills present in the industry of the time that included the talents of those working in front of the camera and, behind the camera, a set of highly talented scriptwriters. What emerges is a veritable network of individual talents that contributed to her emergence as a film star. The label generally applied to Loren's comedies is 'pink neorealism' (*neorealismo rosa*), films of muted social comment that emerged in the period

Table 1: Screen appearances 1952–55.

Film title	First screened
The White Slave Trade	25 September 1952 (as Sofia Lazzaro)
Africa Beneath the Seas	20 March 1953 (as Sophia Loren)
Aida	23 October 1953
Let's Meet in the Gallery	6 November 1953
A Day in Court	13 January 1954
Two Nights with Cleopatra	4 February 1954
A Slice of Life	16 March 1954
Poverty and Nobility	8 April 1954
Neapolitan Carousel	1 October 1954
Pilgrims of Love	11 October 1954
The Gold of Naples	3 December 1954
Attila	27 December 1954
Too Bad She's Bad	28 December 1954
The Woman of the River	29 December 1954
The Sign of Venus	12 March 1955
The Miller's Beautiful Wife	27 October 1955
Scandal in Sorrento	27 December 1955
Lucky to Be a Woman	30 December 1955

Source: Bernardini (1992), *Il cinema sonoro 1930–1969*, Rome: Anica.

1952–7. The grouping subdivides into two distinct sub-genres, largely determined by location: a series of 'rustic comedies', and productions with the urban setting of Rome, labelled films of the 'Roman Arcadia' (D'Amico 1985: 68). Loren's career evolved in direct relation to this, the dominant pattern of Italian comedy in the early to mid-1950s.

Italian comedy films
A fuller picture of the context of Loren's film-making emerges from a second listing, this time setting her key productions (marked with an asterisk) alongside other major comedies of the period[2] (Table 2).

The data in Table 2 demonstrate that the work of Loren and De Sica was an integral part of the broad-based comedy tradition that followed closely on the waning of postwar neorealism, and flourished throughout the 1950s. The list provides evidence that Loren's career drew momentum from a number of quarters. The so-called rustic comedies in fact began with the almost simultaneous issue of *Two Pennyworth of Hope/Due soldi di speranza* and the *Don Camillo* films. The Castellani film is commonly regarded as leading directly to the *Bread and Love* series: the roles of Antonio (Vincenzo Musolino) and Carmela (Maria Fiore) establish the pattern as the rustic couple whose romance is 'blocked' by the girl's father, the standard old man/senex role of classical 'new

Table 2: Key productions (*) and other major comedies of the period.

Film title	Director	Production company	First screened
Don Camillo	Duvivier	Cines/Rizzoli	15 March 1952
Two Pennyworth of Hope	Castellani	Universalcine	10 April 1952
In Olden Days	Blasetti	Cines	28 September 1952
The Return of Don Camillo	Duvivier	Rizzoli Films/Ariane/Rizz	23 September 1953
Bread, Love and Dreams	Comencini	Titanus	22 December 1953
*A Slice of Life	Blasetti	Lux/Cines	16 March 1954
*The Gold of Naples	De Sica	Ponti–De Laurentiis	3 December 1954
*Too Bad She's Bad	Blasetti	Documento Film	28 December 1954
Bread, Love and Jealousy	Comencini	Titanus	6 December 1954
*The Sign of Venus	Risi	Titanus	12 March 1955
Don Camillo's Last Round	Gallone	Francinex/Rizzoli	30 September 1955
*The Miller's Beautiful Wife	Camerini	Titanus/Ponti–De Laurentis	27 October 1955
*Scandal in Sorrento	Risi	Titanus/SGC Paris	27 December 1955
*Lucky to Be a Woman	Blasetti	Documento/Louvre Films	30 December 1955

Source: Bernardini (1992), *Il cinema sonoro 1930–1969*, Rome: Anica.

comedy' (Frye 1957: 26). It is a point that reinforces the importance of the scriptwriters in this period; it is worth noting that one of the film's main scriptwriters, Ettore Margadonna progresses to be a major script contributor to the Titanus rural comedies. *Don Camillo* started the highly popular series of Franco-Italian co-productions funded on the Italian side by the Rizzoli production company with regular leads being the French comic Fernandel and the Italian Gino Cervi. Both films undertook a lengthy location shooting widely reported in the press, a practice that was to continue with De Sica's *The Gold of Naples*: extensive shooting took place for *Don Camillo* in the village of Brescello near Parma, while Boscotrecase, just south of Naples, is acknowledged in the Castellani production as 'meriting our great thanks for its help in the making of this film'. It is clear from the above listing that Titanus played a major part in setting the trend of 'pink neorealist' films. The box-office success of *Bread, Love and Dreams,* alongside that of *Don Camillo,* encouraged the industry to pursue the commercial potential of like films. Dino Risi, one of the major comedy directors of the period, describes film-making at Titanus as combining a 'strong spirit of adventure' with a well-organized working environment under the meticulous supervision of the studio head, the 'producer-auteur' Goffredo Lombardo (Barlozetti 1980: 41). The studio made good use of its own extensive Farnesina studios in Rome to create the fictitious Southern village of Saliena for the first two films in the series. This served to keep costs down, although as Marcus (1986: 139) notes, some location shooting took place at Castel San Pietro, a hill town in the Lazio area, near Palestrina. The comedy trend of the 1950s featured other key figures: the name of director Alessandro Blasetti recurs frequently in the above grouping. De Sica in fact credits Blasetti with reviving his career in the 1952 episode film, *In Olden Days*, where he was cast for the first time with Gina Lollobrigida in the episode 'The Frine Trial': 'Believe it or not, it looked as if my acting career hadn't much of a future until Blasetti offered me the part in that film as a shifty lawyer from Naples. Before that, as an actor, it really looked as if I was finished' (Faldini and Fofi 1979: 263).[3] Blasetti himself claimed responsibility for pairing Loren and Mastroianni for the first time in *Lucky to Be a Woman*, a partnership revived to even greater success under the directorship of De Sica in the 1960s (Faldini and Fofi 1979: 345).

One of the main aims of this study is to underline the way European stardom differs radically from notions of stardom in Hollywood cinema. This is particularly important when we consider the nature of Italian comedy film-making. Although we can say that the films of the period contributed to the development of Loren as a star, with De Sica as a strong presence in the process, whether they qualify as 'star vehicles' for a particular personality is much more problematic. The term 'star vehicle' pre-supposes a Hollywood agenda: in production, with high costs and salary levels of 'star' remuneration, and in marketing, with extensive and costly pre- and post-production publicity to maximize the impact of the film for the star and the success of the relevant studio or funding company. In Italian comedy by contrast we find a form of film-making characterized by an ensemble effort, markedly less oriented towards emphasizing individual bravura. Admittedly, some productions of the period perhaps merit 'star vehicle' classification: the films of Totò and Alberto Sordi were certainly devised around the very particular persona of the lead actor. But even here funding levels were much more modest; short shooting schedules resulted in a form of quick-fire output that signalled a different relationship between a lead actor, the film-makers and the audience. Totò, for example, was contracted to Rosa films to make eight comedies over a three-year period (Ruffin 2002: 274), and Sordi's filmography in the early 1950s shows a similar level of activity.

Wagstaff highlights two main strands to the subject. His argument focuses on the fortunes of the Spaghetti Westerns, but can be seen as relevant also to comedy material. He identifies the 'seriality' of the film's narrative, consisting of an open-ended formula that allows for many sequels where 'the story can more or less begin again' (Wagstaff 1992: 259). This is an argument entirely appropriate to the *Bread and Love* series, so significant to Loren's career. The films regularly conclude with an indeterminate future for the De Sica character, the police sergeant, which allows for a possible rematch with the female lead, where the role of the ageing policeman retains the potential to disrupt and complicate once again the smooth progress of the young lovers' romance. The familiarity of the formula is further significant to what Wagstaff terms the 'social function' of Italian cinema-going (Wagstaff 1992: 253). He suggests that one must also factor in the intensely social role that cinema-going played in the community in this era: the audience came to the local cinema to watch the film, but the cinema building functioned also as a communal meeting place where they interacted regularly with friends. The familiar formula on the screen allowed for audiences to divide their attention between the two activities, as viewers and as members of the community. This dual function of the local cinema is captured beautifully in Giuseppe Tornatore's *Cinema Paradiso* (1989), where all manner of other activities take place in the cinema beyond the obvious act of watching the film. What is argued for the consumption of the film may also be considered valid for the relationship of the audience to the star. It is clear that Loren (and Totò and Sordi) were available on screen with a remarkable degree of regularity, and in this way the status of their films, and their own status, bore scant resemblance to the more rarified, big-budget screenings of Hollywood stars.

To evaluate fully the Loren–De Sica partnership at this time, there is a further factor that merits comment, the role of scriptwriters in film comedy. In one of the very few analyses of their work, Brunetta identifies them as a grouping central to the genre's success, noting at the same time that many were virtually unknown beyond the confines of Italy, and were afforded little critical acclaim even within Italy itself (Brunetta 1998: 264). It was characteristic of the whole field of film-making at this time that scripts were team efforts that evolved through an intensely collaborative process. Eminent names as diverse as Giorgio Bassani, Alberto Moravia, Tullio Pinelli, and Ennio Flaiano had their origins in a range of other artistic fields including theatre, narrative literature and journalism. They and others collaborated both on the popular genre forms with which Loren is associated, and also on those made by the major auteur directors. Suso Cecchi d'Amico worked with Flaiano on a number of Loren scripts. The scope of their work challenges notions of a division between 'arthouse' and 'popular', as they are also key figures in scripting the films of, respectively, Visconti and Fellini. Lesser known, but crucial to the scriptwriting teams were the names of Ettore Margadonna, Alessandro Continenza, Steno, and the team of Age and Scarpelli,[4] all of whom contributed strongly to this most fertile period of film-making, both comic and popular, within which the Loren–De Sica partnership began to flourish, and the genre they revived together with great success after Loren's Hollywood years.

Loren and De Sica's comedy films

Table 1 shows that Loren's early career developed from a body of films that were produced and distributed rapidly, over an intense two-year period. It becomes clear that, in keeping with the broad lines of pink neorealism, the persona of Loren evolved in direct relation to both the rustic and to the urban groupings. As we shall see, a degree of continuity in Loren's roles is retained between the two, but there is also a strong element of diversification that will be explored when considering the urban films with Mastroianni. Loren's interaction with Vittorio De Sica is of course central to this entire period of comedy film-making, and this chapter will concentrate largely on their work together in the rustic comedies. All standard filmographies record that for Loren the connection to De Sica as director began in 1954 with *The Gold of Naples*, and resumed to great acclaim in 1960 with the making of *Two Women*. In the interim, they are credited as actors working together in front of the camera, with a number of well-established names in the director's role. Information from a range of sources puts a rather different complexion on the matter, and documents newly uncovered from the Central State Archive necessitate a reassessment of the received understanding of their professional relationship. Crucially, the evidence establishes that it was in fact Vittorio De Sica who was responsible for directing a number of Italian comedy films central not only to Loren's career but also to the careers of other important screen figures of the 1950s.

In a retrospective interview on his career De Sica himself makes casual reference to the subject: he states that the early 1950s film *Good Morning Elephant/Buongiorno Elefante* (1951), was 'signed by Gianni Franciolini, but [was a film] which I directed and in which I and my wife, Maria, played the lead roles' (Samuels 1972: 181). In relation to the *Bread and Love* series of films Gina Lollobrigida has acknowledged De Sica's part in their success, arguing that 'the real author of these films is Vittorio De Sica. In them there is all his spirit, his comic sense, his passion' (Faldini and Fofi 1979: 344). Elsewhere it was apparently 'broadly rumoured' that not Dino Risi, but De Sica was the director of *The Sign of Venus* (Chiti and Poppi 1991: 326), while Risi himself is recorded as saying that De Sica 'helped out' (*dava una mano*) in making the film (Barlozetti 1980: 41). Documents lodged in the Central State Archive take the issue much further, to show that De Sica was not simply a substantial contributor but in fact was legally contracted and remunerated as director in films generally attributed to others.[5] De Sica's contract for *Bread, Love and Jealousy*, signed and dated 12 June 1954, includes a clause stating that, 'The film will be shot in Italy, in the Italian language, in strict accordance with the script that has been generally approved by Commendatore De Sica: De Sica will contribute to the definitive form of the script, and will have overall responsibility for directing the film' (ACS/ CL/De Sica). A clause in Gina Lollobrigida's contract for the same film, signed and dated 18 June 1954 gives insight into how the role of actor/director would operate stipulating that, 'Commendatore De Sica will be responsible for explaining to you all the requirements of your part, just as he did in *Bread, Love and Dreams*'. The contract shows that Lollobrigida herself was also invited to contribute stating, 'we are happy to include in the script of this second film the comments you have made about the first draft. In so doing we hope to enhance the artistic quality of your role and of the film in general. Where it is judged to be necessary, we are happy to accept further adjustments to the script that may be commonly agreed' (ACS/CL/ Lollobrigida).

The contracts of Loren and De Sica for the third film of the series *Scandal in Sorrento*, signed and dated respectively 3 March 1955 and 10 May 1955, echo strongly the terms of the agreement with Lollobrigida. De Sica's established that 'the film will be shot in Italy, in the Italian language, in accordance with any necessary revisions to the script authorised by Vittorio De Sica, along with other collaborators. Commendatore De Sica will co-direct the film, but without formal recognition of his directorial role' (ACS/CL/De Sica); Loren's specifies that 'the said film will list Dino Risi as director, but the supervisor of direction will be Vittorio De Sica who, it is agreed, will be present, as in all the preceding films, at all times when you are required to be on camera' (ACS/CL/Loren). The content of these contracts gives a most remarkable insight into the film-making process for Loren, De Sica and Lollobrigida. Firstly it underlines the collaborative nature of the film scripting. While Margadonna is credited with devising the broad lines (*soggetto*) of the comic formula in the original and the later films, the actors' contracts for the second film show that the actual script (*scenaggiatura*) was an on-going process, possibly continuing during shooting itself. De Sica, it is suggested, will contribute to 'the definitive form of the script' (ACS/CL/De Sica), but Lollobrigida's contract shows a considerable degree of flexibility as to what 'definitive' might mean: the wording, as we see, allows for 'further adjustments to the script that may be commonly agreed' (ACS/CL/Lollobrigida). But secondly and most importantly, we find in Loren's contract additional information regarding her partnership with De Sica that reinforces the importance of his role in developing her acting skills. The requirement of De Sica to be present 'in all the scenes when [Loren] is on camera' (ACS/CL/ Loren) appears to draw them even closer professionally, to give grounds for asserting even more forcefully that she made her beginnings as his on-screen creation. But the latter section of the clause concludes with a stipulation that requires us to amend such a perspective. It records that this is a role already carried out by De Sica 'in all the preceding films' (ACS/CL/Loren). I take this to mean 'all the preceding films of the *Bread and Love* series': the connection is reinforced by additional wording, repeated in the papers for all three artists that 'it is expressly forbidden to make any mention of the fact that De Sica is director of this film, a condition imposed also in the contracts for *Bread, Love and Dreams*' (ACS/CL/De Sica, Lollobrigida, Loren). This surely prompts much broader conclusions regarding the films' authorship. What transpires is, instead, that input to Loren's career was merely part of De Sica's much more comprehensive role in directing, scripting and acting across the whole body of work: as such, it is more valid to register him as the driving force behind the efforts of *all* those involved in the series. Besides Loren, Gina Lollobrigida is naturally the most prominent but by no means the only artist deriving benefit from De Sica's creative input. The series sustained the careers of wide-ranging technical crew members, cameramen and scriptwriters: at the same time character actors such as Tina Pica, Peppino De Filippo and Mimmo Carotenuto, largely unacknowledged as a mainstay of the postwar comic genre, featured repeatedly in the casting, and were again in support when Loren and De Sica returned to comedy film-making in the 1960s.

Documentation from the urban comedy *The Sign of Venus*, more fully considered in Chapter 5, is also relevant here. The archive file of the film contains a letter dated 12 November 1954 from producer Gustavo Lombardo to Nicola De Pirro, chair of the committee awarding state funding. In the letter Lombardo points out that Dino Risi is identified on the cast listing as director of the film, and he continues, 'I have to tell you in strictest confidence that the director is in fact Vittorio De Sica whose name, for various reasons, we do not want to enter on the document' (ACS/ MV/*The Sign of Venus*). Risi's name is thus to be used as what Lombardo terms a 'cover' (*un prestanome*) to conceal the true identity of the director. Why were such elaborate efforts made to conceal De Sica's authorship of these important films? The question cannot be fully pursued here, but a few salient points may be noted. In his letter to De Pirro, Lombardo goes on to suggest that, 'the reason that De Sica does not openly accept authorship of the film is that the public would expect him to produce an *Umberto D*-type film. By using Risi's name as a cover he can put into this new film all his humane and dramatic creativity which, as a good Neapolitan, he has in abundance' (ACS/MV/*The Sign of Venus*). Lombardo's meaning here is not altogether clear, but it appears to suggest the view that, in shedding the heavy mantle of his neorealist work, De Sica can more freely operate as a comedic film-maker. The point must be understood in relation to the contradictory status of De Sica's film-making at the time. While internationally renowned for his neorealist films, he was the target of hostility on the part of the Italian political establishment, and had been openly denounced by leading Christian Democrat Giulio Andreotti on the grounds that if the public were to believe the image of Italy presented in his films, 'De Sica will have rendered a very bad service to his country' (quoted in Forgacs 1989: 64). Lombardo may be suggesting that by transferring his energies to a different type of film-making, De Sica no longer carries the burden of possible further attacks on him by the establishment. Other commentators attest to De Sica's difficulties with his professional and personal finances. His wife Maria Mercader charts the struggle to pay off debts that he incurred in making *Sciuscià* (1946) and *Bicycle Thieves* (1948) recounting that, weary of the constant hunt for funding, De Sica eventually resolved to continue his film-making, but thereafter in films 'funded by other people's money' (Mercader: 2002). Additionally, funds were needed to support the director's difficult marital circumstances, and, it is alleged, his considerable gambling habits (Cardullo 2002: 59).[6] We have already noted the customary reluctance of critics to give due critical attention to popular film-making; but over and above this, the consensus remains that De Sica's work in comedy is inferior to his neorealist output and that, following *Umberto D*, he entered a stage of his career that has been labelled 'the period of commercial compromise' (Cardullo 2002: 56). This new documentation underlines the need for a re-evaluation of the place of comedy film-making in De Sica's long career. It gives further impetus to the assertion implicit in the critical cannon that neorealism forms the dominant narrative of postwar Italian cinema is in fact a perspective that should investigated with much greater rigour. Galt rightly argues that the tendency to accept neorealism as the central pathway by which all subsequent films must position themselves is one that 'should not be accepted without pause' (Galt 2006: 74). It is highly likely that the archive evidence set out in this chapter regarding De Sica's involvement in directing and scriptwriting was common knowledge throughout the industry of the time, and must have been self-evident to those working with him directly on set. However, it is a subject that is yet to receive due critical attention, with the resultant gaps in a full understanding of the careers of Loren, Lollobrigida and De Sica himself. It is certainly worth repeating here the opinion of David Ellwood that it is in these very comedies, rather than in neorealism, that the spirit of postwar Italy is best articulated (Ellwood 1999: 826). At the very least, the terms of the artists' contracts provide a more solid basis for assessing the workings of several comedy partnerships.

Scandal in Sorrento: Adapting and promoting the formula
There is no doubt that De Sica's *The Gold of Naples*, released in December 1954, was a key film in establishing Loren as the shapely Neapolitan star, and associations with the provincial or rural setting were to remain significant to her star image throughout her career. However, the Neapolitan dimension had already been actively pursued in films that pre-date the De Sica film. She was frequently cast with the Neapolitan comedy actor Totò: she played joint lead with him in the five-minute episode entitled 'The Camera' (*La macchina fotografica*) of Blasetti's *A Slice of Life* (released March 1954), a bit part in Mattoli's *Poverty and Nobility* (released April 1954) where Totò has the lead role. She took the part of the elegant chorus girl Sisina in an episode of Giannini's *Neapolitan Carousel* (released October 1954), and she and Totò were then cast in separate episodes of *The Gold of Naples* that had its premiere in December of the same year. The trend is not subsequently pursued in *The Miller's Beautiful Wife*, which is only very vaguely referenced as taking part in a Southern Italian location in the nineteenth century, during the period of Spanish rule. However, once Loren was finally confirmed as lead in the third *Bread and Love* film, the producers Titanus planned and carried out modifications to the generic formula based on associations with the Naples area. Though triggered by the necessity of replacing Lollobrigida as lead, the changes were nevertheless in other ways typical of the evolution of a genre form where producers continually seek a balance between the audience's demand for novelty, while at the same time protecting their investment by relying on established conventions with proven commercial success (Schatz 1981: 25). Part of the draw of this third film was most certainly the interest in seeing how Loren might perform in a role so closely

associated with another major star. Titanus clearly assessed Loren's box-office potential as sufficient to make considerable investment in pre-production and publicity planning.

For the third film the location shifted from the fictitious village of Saliena to the actual location of Sorrento; this specifically signalled a more Loren-related orientation in that it referenced her place of origin, the nearby Pozzuoli, as well as reinforcing the Naples connection already established in her preceding films. The shooting schedule shows that there was to be extensive location work in Sorrento and the surrounding area (six weeks) with only very brief use (one week) of the Farnesina studios in Rome (ACS/PL/*Scandal in Sorrento*). This showed that that the studio was confident of recouping what was bound to be a more costly enterprise, and the budget costs of the films shows the steadily increasing outlay that the studio undertook with regard to this series of films (Appendix B: Archive Sample 3). Ahead of filming, Gustavo Lombardo even authorized a competition to 'name the film', where the prize was a trip to Sorrento to be present during shooting on the set.[7] The use of a location proffered as even remotely synonymous with Loren was, of course, decidedly false. *The Gold of Naples*, though hardly offering a fully realist perspective on the city, captured some valid associations with the setting in its lighter aspects (particularly Loren's own 'Pizza on Credit' episode) and the darker moments (the obsessive quality of De Sica's card-playing character in 'The Gambler', the abject defeat of Teresa, the prostitute figure played by Silvana Mangano) as a more nuanced representation of the character of the locale and its inhabitants. The setting of *Scandal in Sorrento* is decidedly sanitized, a tourist-eye's perspective repeated with even greater insistence in the Capri of the later Paramount-produced *It Started in Naples*. Loren's role bears little resemblance either to the real-life experience of a widowed fishmonger of the area or even to her own difficult beginnings in Pozzuoli. But this was rarely the point of the rural comedies: indeed any attempt at equating the tenor of the *Bread and Love* series with the social underpinning of the original neorealism (suggested by the 'pink neorealism' label), is at best extremely tenuous.

At the box office the film slightly underperformed in relation to the first two films of the series, but for Loren, the entire project was a triumph that confirmed her ascendancy as one of the shapely stars, stepping literally into Lollobrigida's shoes. It fed further notions of rivalry between them that were recounted in many inches of newspaper and magazine columns. It is particularly interesting that it is as Donna Sofia that Loren first features on the cover of *Life* on 22 August 1955, with the caption 'Europe's no. 1 cover girl: Sophia Loren as fishmonger in new Italian film', reinforcing that her construction as star in the United States differed substantially from the evolution of her Italian stardom: the film itself was not in fact released in the US until May 1957, where it had little commercial impact. The film *Bread, Love and Andalusia/Pane amore e Andalusia* (Setó, 1959), a joint Spanish–Italian collaboration, involving De Sica's own production company De Sica Films, brought the series to an end where only he remained from the original acting leads. As we shall see in Chapter 5, thereafter contemporary Italian comedy was marked by a radical change in gender representation with a shift to male stars, and narratives where preoccupations of masculinity predominated (Gunsberg 2005: 73). The careers of the 'shapely stars' were to evolve in a range of ways: Loren to Hollywood, Lollobrigida abandoning comedy to star in a number of costly European and American-funded melodramas, while Mangano largely withdrew all together from popular film-making, and only occasionally undertook work mainly with arthouse directors Visconti and Pasolini.

The broad lines of *Scandal in Sorrento* perpetuated and brought to a conclusion the association, begun in *Bitter Rice*, of linking an assertive female physicality with the rural. It was an important location for the shapely stars, allowing a form of dress, (supposedly peasant, supposedly that of a working local girl) designed to emphasize their 'curvaceous fleshy bodies, little tummies, full lips and expressive eyes' (Wood 2005: 166). It was a context deemed to give licence to express a powerful sexuality, whether through the medium of melodrama (*Bitter Rice, The Woman of the River* and *The Ricefield*) or the comedy of the *Bread and Love* series. Throughout, dance is retained as a means to express this freedom, and as social changes were wrought in 1950s Italy, so one notes a progressive representation of the destabilizing potential of female sexuality. It originates in the boogie-woogie of Mangano but as we have seen the film concludes in her death, and the social norm is re-established through her elimination from the narrative. The *Bread and Love* series indirectly references elements of this original, and in the first two films Lollobrigida undertakes some light-hearted dance routines. In the third film Loren's performance is even more provocative. She dances a mambo in the town square in a red, figure-hugging dress with body language at once comic but also almost orgiastic in tone. It is she who invites the police sergeant Carotenuto (De Sica) to dance: ostensibly the aim is to provoke her young jealous suitor Nicolino (Antonio Cifariello) who is already on the dance floor paired with a blond tourist girl. In the extended sequence that follows the camera gradually isolates the Loren figure who begins to dance alone with eyes half-closed, increasingly oblivious to and independent of the male partners, young and old, positioned at the margins of the shots were she is centred. The harmonious conclusion required by comic conventions is honoured as she eventually rejoins Carotenuto to bring the mambo routine to a close: re-establishing the pairing suggests that the sexual power of the female partner is once again contained, part of the process of stabilization of social relationships that traditionally concludes the comic narrative. However, such a conclusion is considerably undermined by the erotic charge of Loren's on-screen movement and presence. Reich (2004: 33) identifies these qualities as part of the image of Loren as the 'unruly woman' that begins to evolve at this time: the detail of this image, taken in combination with the urban setting, will be fully explored in analysis of the Loren and Mastroianni partnership in Chapter 5.

Case study: Two Women

Following the conclusion of the *Bread and Love* series, the partnership of Loren as actress and De Sica as director shows a five-year hiatus. While Loren worked with Mastroianni and Blasetti on two further comedies, and then progressed to the Hollywood phase of her career, De Sica was himself involved in a number of projects as director, some abortive, with Hollywood studios (Samuels 1972: 186), and also undertook a demanding acting schedule in a range of national and international productions. By July 1960, when shooting *Two Women* began, Loren's screen career was faltering: much rode on its potential to re-establish her on-screen credentials. Reviving the partnership with De Sica was certainly an important part of the process. The film proved to be the high point of their collaboration, winning many awards, all specific to Loren as best actress that indicated unanimous approval across a wide range of spectator groups.[8] Exceptionally, it was a success marked by both commercial and critical approval. Ponti himself was convinced that 'fifty per cent of Sophia's career success derived from the Oscar she won for that film' (Della Casa 2003: 84) (Figure 4). *Two Women* has been extensively analysed

Figure 4: Sophia, Ponti and Lombardo celebrate her Oscar as Best actress for *Two Women*. Stills Department, Cineteca Nazionale, Rome.

both as an individual film (Marcus 1993: 67–90; Nerenberg 2004: 242–69; McIntyre 2000: 242–57) and in relation to its place in De Sica's directorial career (Cardullo 2002; Price 2000). However, little emphasis has been given to the significance of the role played by aspects of the production, promotion and publicity in bringing about the film's success. What is more, despite the particular acclaim given to Loren herself, few attempts have been made to assess the quality of her performance in the film. Questions of performance in cinema are acknowledged to be particularly problematic: the very term 'performance', deriving from theatrical terminology, is less easily applied to film. As De Cordova (1991: 120), argues, in cinema performance comes about through the combination of the actor who enacts a part, and the cinematic apparatus that shapes and conveys that enactment to the audience. In assessing performance in cinema it remains important to consider the interaction of performer and audience while at the same time acknowledging that, in contrast to the theatre, the audience does not participate in a live performance. The case study will show that at the time of the release of *Two Women* audiences and critics engaged in a very particular way with Loren's persona and in so doing actively contributed to reinvigorating her star status.

Promotion and publicity
In the chapter on Loren and Hollywood extensive consideration was given to the question of 'leakage' between promotional strategies, pre-planned and executed, and less controlled, exposé-type publicity, and the relevance of this issue to Loren's early career. The matter arises

again very strongly in relation to *Two Women* where it is clear that elements shaping Loren's success in the film began well before production plans were finalized. The making of the film was billed as part of the star's return to Italy, but the notion of 'return' requires more careful investigation. The phase termed her 'Hollywood' career had in fact, as already noted, concluded in Europe with filming in Vienna of *A Breath of Scandal* (Curtiz, 1960), co-financed by Paramount and Titanus, and the last Paramount film *It Started in Naples* (Shavelson, 1960), shot in Capri with co-star Clark Gable. Funding for both films reverted to the practices of Loren's earlier runaway productions, drawing on Paramount's blocked funds, the company's box-office profits in Italy. In a tight schedule reminiscent of the intensive output of pre-Hollywood days, she then transferred from Capri to London where she completed filming *The Millionairess* with Peter Sellers and director Anthony Asquith; by the time the film premiered in London in October 1960 shooting for the De Sica film was already well advanced. In a very real sense, therefore, Loren's had already relocated back to Europe and initially one can see that her off-screen activities generated much more press interest than these films, that instead received a very lukewarm commercial and critical response. Scrutiny of popular publications of the period makes clear that there were in fact several strands to Loren's relationship with the press that, overall, had a largely positive effect on her career. The very sympathic tenor of reports on her marriage, where sections of the press defended her against her treatment by officialdom, has been highlighted. While the legal position was debated in the Italian courts, the 'exile' of Loren and Ponti remained in place, but perhaps somewhat paradoxically it appears that this absence from Italy served rather to enhance her star persona. Whatever her personal distress, she and Ponti were clearly not harmed financially by the matter. They had for some time set up home is Switzerland, and now established residence also in Paris. Loren's persona continued to draw on her Italian identity, but increasingly this formed only a part of her meaning as star. Hers was by this time an image in considerable flux: while cinemagoers, public and press continued to register the impact of Hollywood on her star image, that image was modified again in a process of re-orientation towards European stardom.[9] The potential for future on-screen success remained unclear, but renewal of her status in Europe takes a number of interesting forms.

Firstly, Loren became increasingly visible on the European celebrity circuit. She maintained a regular, glittering presence at European Film Festivals, both at Cannes and Berlin, and at events such as the premiere in London of her film with Sellers. The events were widely recorded in shots staged for an attendant press, and used to ensure maximum publicity for Loren's work. Where earlier appearances had been quite tentative, tied to her career beginnings, she now became one of the defining presences at celebrity functions. *Gente* reported her as hosting a glamorous yacht party at Cannes in May 1959, attended by Ponti, producer Angelo Rizzoli and other personalities from the film world (Peverelli 1959: 8–12), while in the following month her appearance at the Berlin Film Festival was widely reported. In what was billed as an 'investigative report on the stars' undertaken by the journalist and writer Giuseppe Marotta, we find in fact a lengthy quasi-promotional exercise lavishly illustrated with shots of Loren at the event, where she is presented, bejewelled and in designer gowns, dancing, dining and signing autographs in the most elegant company (Marotta 1959: 23–7). While these examples might most probably be labelled 'publicity', they surely served a useful promotional purpose. Despite the carefree air of such shots, commentators have argued that a star's attendance at festivals could be viewed as an essential part of the job, with a punishing round of interviews and appearances, coupled with the requirement to be constantly available and always impeccably groomed (Beauchamp and Behar 1992: 186). Loren was certainly recognized as one of the most assiduous participants on the festival circuit and eventually led the jury of the Cannes Film Festival in 1966 (Corless and Darke 2007: 103). As far as links with the fashion world were concerned, an even more direct strategy emerged, in the form of a series of contracts between Loren and various European couturiers.

Fashion and cinema had long been an important facet of Hollywood tradition where, in the studio era, magazines published detailed accounts of what individual stars wore in specific films, and even issued patterns that enabled the public to emulate the star's appearance. Now, in the 1950s, European fashion houses seized the initiative as they too began to mass-market their products, marking a further shift away from Hollywood domination in cinema and its attendant industries. As Elizabeth Wilson has observed (1993: 38) the situation was certainly beneficial to European stars, as well as other leading personalities involved in European film-making. Wilson cites the example of Audrey Hepburn in *Sabrina* (Wilder, 1954) where the power of European fashion is an explicit feature of the narrative, as it features Hepburn's transformation from shy teenager to a poised figure elegantly garbed in Givenchy gowns (Wilson 1997: 41). In Italy similar links were evident: the Rome-based studio of the Fontana sisters designed Hepburn's wardrobe in Wyler's 1953 production *Roman Holiday*, and the costumes of Ava Gardner in *The Barefoot Contessa* (Mankewicz, 1954), both filmed in Italy. Couturier Emile Schuberth, also based in Rome, had a long association with Loren and Lollobrigida; he is credited as designer of Loren's wardrobe as the aspiring fashion model in *Lucky to Be a Woman,* and provided the gowns, extensively photographed, when she first travelled to Los Angeles in 1957. Reka Buckley shows that Italian designers became increasingly popular in this period, and thus contributed extensively to a fresh image for individual stars, and for the reputation of Italy as a leading presence in the image of Europe and European fashion (Buckley 2008: 267–89). Loren, domiciled partly in Switzerland and partly in Paris, now took up a contract with Yves St Laurent at Dior, a move that surely underscored for her a more European orientation. *Jours de France* showcased the designs in a seven-page spread with the headline 'Sophie la Parisienne' (Fournal and Tikhomioff 1960: 28–34) that loosely translates as 'Sophia, Parisian style'. This move supports the view that in this period Loren had become an 'ambassador of elegance and beauty, marked by a style regarded highly from Paris to Rome to New York' (Anon (e) 1959): but *Oggi's* anonymous commentator still appears to take Loren's style as enhancing the reputation of Italy, even as her sponsorship of fashion products moved elsewhere.[10]

Irrespective of whether these were part of a unified promotional campaign or simply a series of individual reporting opportunities, Loren remained the subject of a number of carefully staged, high-profile reports. When she travelled from Vienna to Rome in June 1959 to complete the filming of *A Breath of Scandal,* headlines such as 'Torno in Italia, magari in galera (I'm determined to go back to Italy, even if I have to go to jail)' (Guidi 1959: 23) and 'Torno in Italia con il cuore in gola (I'm returning to Italy, with my heart in my mouth)' (Sansa 1959: 10) were common. In the latter report the written text is amply illustrated with shots of a perfectly posed Loren, immaculately dressed and coiffed, packing suitcases in a hotel room, then waving from a train window with an appropriately anxious look on her face; it is a scenario that one may assume was created largely, if not solely, for the benefit of the magazine's press photographer, duly summoned to present a most sympathetic portrayal of Loren. A year later, when Loren arrived to shoot *Two Women*, a more sustained campaign was set in motion. Shortly after her plane landed in Rome, the agency of Spinola and Lucherini was hired to handle her relationship with the press (Lucherini and Spinola 1984: 43), and Pier Luigi Praturlon was appointed official photographer to the film. It was a role Praturlon had previously taken on in 1957, in the runaway production *Legend of the Lost*, but by now he was a major force in Italian cinema where he had recently collaborated extensively with Fellini on *La dolce vita*. According to Spinola, Hollywood practices were now to become an important part of Loren's European activity. He recounts that she followed the lessons learned from American press agents, and that it was he who gained expertise from her, rather than she who took his advice on what materials and information to make available to the press about her activities (Lucherini and Spinola 1984: 49). Both Spinola and Secchiaroli testify to the commanding role that Loren assumed in their collaborations. Tazio Secchiaroli, who succeeded Praturlon as Loren's official photographer in the 1960s films with Mastroianni, is equally adamant as regards Loren's role in his work: with the use of blurred focus and apparently casual poses, he and the actress convinced the press that shots released to them were 'stolen', and of a much more invasive nature, whereas they were in fact taken by Secchiaroli, with the full knowledge and sanction of Loren herself (Bertelli and Secchiaroli 2003: 35).[11]

Reporters were now encouraged to be present on set: this was part of a broader strategy to counter the adverse publicity of Loren's marital difficulties, and popularize her image with the more traditional sectors of the Italian public (Lucherini and Spinola 1984: 42). Again, this emulated a practice rapidly evolving also in Hollywood. When Loren began work on *Desire under the Elms*, *Photoplay* proudly proclaimed an 'exclusive access to the set', with shots of Loren and other members of the cast at work reading and discussing the script (Archer 1957: 21). It was a strategy that revealed the changing relationship between the stars and their audience. In the 1930s and 1940s studios exercised strict control over access to employees, but in an era where there was greater competition for viewers, production companies became aware of the promotional benefit of press interest in the cast of their forthcoming film. While shooting *The Millionairess* in London, some dramatic stills from the film were circulated showing Loren apparently committing suicide (jumping out of a window into the Thames) to stimulate the interest of the timid Doctor Kabir (Peter Sellers). The press were brought on set to take shots exposing the trick that she had in fact landed on a set of cushions strategically placed below the line of the film camera. The *paparazzi* of late 1950s Italy also played an important role in this respect. Revealing shots of stars of Hollywood and non-Hollywood origin had been repeatedly caught on camera by photographers such as Secchiaroli himself, the model for the role of Paparazzo in *La dolce vita*: shots of personalities from Ava Gardner, Walter Chiari and Anita Ekberg, to royalty figures such as exiled King Farouk of Egypt and members of European and Italian aristocracy were part of an era of increasing democratization, that brought the star much closer to his/her public. It is a complex relationship where accusations of the invasiveness of the press are countered, to this day, by the sense that all publicity favours the star image. Within this particular climate, Loren's own profile in the press remained high, but it was yet to be seen whether it would be matched by her on-screen achievement.

The film: Preparation and production strategies

Scripting and production arrangements for Two Women are widely known. The broad lines of the film's narrative (soggetto) were based on Alberto Moravia's novel La ciociara first published in 1957. Cesare Zavattini, collaborator with De Sica on several major neorealist films, took on the task of adapting it for the screen. Again, Ponti showed his eye for a good script by securing the film rights to Moravia's novel shortly after publication. Early reports listed the film as a possible Paramount production (Pryor: 1959), but the plan clearly evaporated as the studio withdrew from involvement in Loren's career. Anna Magnani was originally to be cast in the central role of the mother Cesira, with Loren as her daughter Rosetta. Magnani then withdrew from the project, and the role of Cesira was assigned to Loren, casting that necessitated some major adjustments to the script.[12] The team of De Sica and Zavattini combined with a film crew consisting of highly experienced practitioners, Gastone Medin as set designer, Gabor Pogany as chief cameraman, Armando Trovaioli in charge of music, and Adriana Novelli as editor. Unlike Praturlon or Secchiaroli, none of them was particularly well known in their own right, but they had each developed a long and successful working association with De Sica. The film is registered as a French–Italian co-production that qualified, as was the usual practice, for both French and Italian state funding (ACS/PF/Two Women), where the casting of the rising French star Jean-Paul Belmondo as the radical young teacher Michele justified the French subsidy. Titanus, for long producer of a number of Loren–De-Sica films, was now involved solely as Italian distributor; US distribution rights were negotiated by Embassy Pictures, through Joe Levine, and the significance of Levine for the film's international success will be considered later in the chapter. Analysis of the film's central episode is ideal for an assessment of Loren's performance in this case study. It is made up of three sequences shot in separate locations: the rape of the two women in an abandoned church, the aftermath of the rape where, on a mountainous roadside, they meet a jeep carrying three Allied officials, and a final sequence when Cesira follows her daughter down the valley to wash in a mountain stream. The episode in the church is the most shocking point of the narrative and has rightly received close attention (Marcus: 1993), but the focus here will be on the roadside sequence, of equal importance as a measure of Loren's performance. For the analysis I shall draw not only on the sequence itself, but also on De Sica's written notes for the film, Letters from the Set (Lettere dal set).

The cinematic apparatus

Letters from the Set consists of material covering three Loren–De Sica films: Two Women (1960), Yesterday, Today and Tomorrow (1963) and Marriage Italian Style (1964). The letters referred to in the title were written by De Sica to his daughter Emi during production of the films. As he began the first set of letters for Two Women in July 1960, De Sica expressed the hope that they might be collected together to form a film diary, and Emi De Sica finally oversaw publication of the material with the specific purpose of paying homage to her father's memory (De Sica and Governi 1987: 8). De Sica's writings give considerable insight into his method of working on set. Filming took place almost entirely on location, the shooting planned out to include one week in Rome (in Trastevere, and at Termini and Tiburtina railway stations); four weeks based in Formia in the Ciociaria area; four weeks in Saracinesco, near Tivoli; and a final two weeks in Rome (AS/PL/Two Women).[13] Both Moravia and De Sica relied on close personal knowledge of the main location for shooting, the Ciocaria region: in the winter of 1943–4 Moravia had lived in the central town of Fondi as a refugee from the Nazi occupation of Rome, while De Sica was born in the town of Sora to the north-east of the area, though within a few years the family moved to Naples. De Sica's shooting retains the quality of Moravia's original text that maps out the journey of Cesira and Rosetta in close detail, citing locations scattered throughout this mountainous region between Rome and Naples. Located near the strategic site of Monte Cassino, it was an area of fierce fighting between the retreating German forces and the advancing Allied troops. For a time Emi De Sica worked as a production assistant on her father's films, and this may partly explain the emphasis taken by De Sica in his letters, where he gives her a detailed account of the experience of shooting the film. The dominant aspect of De Sica's work, at least as far as he conveys it to his daughter, is found not so much in efforts to direct the cast, but in a relentless drive to find the locations most suited to filming particular sequences.

In this respect, the division of labour is quite clear. De Sica himself takes the task of establishing suitable exterior locations and, once these are identified, he assigns preparation of the interiors (of the church, for example) to the designated production designer Gastone Medin (LS, August 1: 59). His approach is well exemplified in the shooting of the central episode. After a week's shooting in Rome with Loren and Raf Vallone (in the role of Giovanni), cast and crew moved to a base in Formia, on the coastal edge of the Ciociaria area. By this time De Sica reports that he had already undertaken numerous journeys to research the mountainous inland area. The central episode is presented in the film in the same logical chronology as that of the written text, progressing from the terrible events in the church, to the meeting with the Allied officials by the roadside, to the concluding sequence by the stream. De Sica's diary shows that the order of shooting was quite different: Cesira's meeting with the officials was the first to be shot, on 31 July (LS: 57); then, while still based in Formia, the sequence at the church was filmed over four days from 16 August to 20 August (LS: 71), and the final sequence, at the river, was shot much later on 23 September, when the crew transferred to Saracinesco (LS: 95). The sequence at the roadside was thus given priority, following immediately on the transfer from Rome to Formia, a decision explained by De Sica in this way:

> The site that I have chosen is well suited to the scene. I had to find a match that would link it with what follows in the narrative, the events that take place at the stream which instead I intend to shoot later, when we transfer to Saracinesco. It consists of a narrow valley cut down the middle by a deep ditch. The walls of the two mountains that frame the valley are grey and dark, which serves to make the scene even more dramatic. Sofia is worried because it is a very difficult scene. But I instead have no doubt that she will make a success of it. She is an actress who, with guidance and good direction, is capable of giving a great performance. At this stage I don't know what kind of film I will eventually produce. Maybe it will have a slightly dated quality, given the nature of the material it covers, but irrespective of this Sofia's role will be one of the greatest that an actress can possibly hope to play (LS , 31 July: 57).

The comment on the suitability of the scene suggests De Sica had the specifics of Moravia's novel directly in mind, and the finished piece gives particular justification to the decision to shoot the film in black and white. In the written narrative, presented through Cesira's eyes, she describes the road as 'bare, deserted, and glinting, like a snake twisting and turning in the sun' (Moravia 1957: 255). Thus the film setting appears precisely as suggested in the written text: the key events take place beside a small bridge, where Cesira and Rosetta pause to rest, and the bridge is situated at a bend on a descending valley road with twisting contours that, coupled with the folds of the grey, bare mountains give bold, sweeping definition to the location. De Sica's meticulous research is of central importance in establishing the setting for Loren's enactment of the part. Equally significant are the editing and use of camera, the dominant characteristics of the finished episode: the quick editing gives a sense of movement, created not by the figures on the screen, who are largely static, but by a range of different camera positions rapidly edited together. The camerawork includes a series of conventional medium shot/reverse shots between Cesira and the soldiers on the jeep, the standard presentation used to convey exchanges (of information, feelings) within a group, but this pattern is interspersed strikingly with long shots that apparently present a point of view, but where ownership of the point-of-view is never established. In rapid succession the audience is offered shots of mother and daughter, the camera being positioned above, below and at a lateral angle to characters on the descending valley road. Some shots are taken from behind the grouping of the women and the jeep, others show the figures, especially Cesira, face-on to the camera. The camera frames the figures mainly in medium shot: either singly (Cesira), in pairs (Cesira and Rosetta) or in various combinations of the soldiers, Cesira and Rosetta, all the while constantly shifting position around the figures. In addition, long shots are used to set the women against the mountains, making them look small and highlighting further their vulnerability, already acutely evident in the sequence at the church. The destabilizing effect of the camerawork is carefully attuned to the meaning of the narrative at this point, a literal manifestation of the problem of how the figure of Cesira may now be framed. She must shed the illusory role she has assumed as protector to her daughter, and acknowledge the inevitability of the impact of war (Marcus 1993: 73). But how Cesira will survive the blow is not clear, even at the end of the film. Her daughter has effectively prostituted herself to Florindo (Renato Salvatori) and the final shot of the film simply shows with uncertain emphasis the figures of mother and daughter travelling back to Rome in Florindo's truck.

The pace of the narrative accelerates as Cesira steps up from the bridge to stop the jeep. She confronts the three officials it contains, accusing them of responsibility for the rape, for failing to control the soldiers under their command. The individual in the back of the jeep, anxious to press on, signals to his fellow-officers with a finger pointing at his head to suggest that Cesira is mad, and does not merit any more of their time. She responds, shouting 'No, I'm not mad', and picks up a stone to threaten them. The jeep takes off rapidly down the valley road, and she turns and throws the stone towards it, a gesture at once defiant and by now futile, all the while observed silently by her daughter Rosetta. Overwhelmed by the moment, by the attack in the church and by the war, Cesira huddles down on one knee as her daughter exits the shot to climb down, as the viewer later learns, to the stream. At this juncture of the film, the mode of performance is best described as 'histrionic', that is ostentatious, excessive and marked by heavily stressed gestures (Stern 1999: 108). It is worth underlining again that the overall effect of the scene is one of nervous, uncertain movement achieved through camerawork: in contrast, the characters on camera remain largely immobile. The figure of Loren is as if rooted to the spot, a detail well linked to the fear and trauma of the part; even her gestures are few – restricted to stretching out her arm towards Rosetta, to show her daughter's plight to the soldiers. The enactment is intensely theatrical, and this is achieved largely through stance, the defiant stand of a ragged, dishevelled woman facing the uncomprehending officers, themselves motionless and decidedly indifferent to the women's plight. The performance culminates in the moment when, following the fruitless gesture of throwing the stone, the isolated, abandoned figure of Cesira crumples down, half kneeling on the road. It is an iconic moment rendered in long shot that emphasizes the empty, unforgiving landscape around her. Its power is attributable firstly to the moving camera of Gabor Pogany, and then also to the still camera of the official on-set photographer Pier Luigi Praturlon. Disseminated around the world, by means of the film, magazine covers and most recently the film's DVD cover, it is the definitive image of Loren's career.

Performance: Meaning and reception

A sample review is sufficient to show the broad lines of the critical response to Loren's performance. In La settimana incom of 12 August 1960 we find the comment:

> This is a very important film for Sophia Loren because at last it gives her the chance to show off her qualities and potential to the best advantage, with the result that Two Women is indubitably her best film. The film is important because it compensates her substantially for all the missed opportunities in the many productions she made outside Italy, that were completely unsuited to her skills as an actress.

In the simplest terms, Two Women appeared to convince public and critics that 'Loren can act'. As observed in Chapter 2, the view that the shapely Italian stars could not act was broadly adopted by commentators of weighty cinema journals such as Cinema nuovo. This was a perspective neither unique to Loren, nor to the wider spectrum of other like stars of the period. The British starlet Diana Dors experienced similar treatment, though this time at the hands of the tabloid press, who, even within a positive review, 'invariably registered surprise that a sex symbol should manifest any acting ability at all' (Cook 2001: 167). Loren was a more popular, and much more commercially successful star than Dors, but the dismissive view that their success was entirely dependent on their shapely bodies was common. With Two Women, Loren made a return not to comedy, the generic form that had defined her popularity in the pre-Hollywood years, but to melodrama, a choice that influenced directly the estimation of her acting ability. The move was judicious: De Cordova (1991: 122) argues that, more than any other genre, melodrama has supported the claim that film incorporates the art of acting. He takes the point further, arguing that the fictional material of melodrama often concerns the topics of suffering, hysteria and madness, where 'a character's mental disturbance in the fiction is accompanied at the level of enunciation by the placement of the actor in a number of strongly marked scenes of performance' (De Cordova 1991: 122). De Cordova cites examples from the Hollywood films of Nicholas Ray and Elia Kazan, but his comments clearly have the closest relevance to the performance of Loren in the roadside sequence: its meaning is underpinned precisely with the possibility that the horror of war will drive Cesira to madness. It is a subject already broached in the film in an earlier scene when she and Michele visit Fondi, and encounter a crazed young woman, Lena, who has lost her baby in the war and wanders the ruins of the village offering her lactating breast to passers-by.

Both Marcus (1993: 24) and Nerenberg (2004: 93) express concern that there may be an element of racism or needless stereotyping in the ethnic orientation assigned in the novel and in the film to the attacking soldiers. It is therefore important to emphasize that this fictitious central episode of the rape of Cesira and Rosetta is based on real-life atrocities documented in two main sources. Incidences of rape by Moroccan soldiers are recorded in *Naples '44*, the war diary of Norman Lewis, based on the author's first-hand experiences that includes an account of his meeting with 'a girl said to have been driven insane by a large party of Moors' (Lewis 2002: 131); and James Holland's recent detailed account of the final year of the war in Italy draws on the testimony of a number of women of the Ciocaria brutalized during the war, whose accounts Holland traced in archive files held in Rome. The part thus requires Loren to articulate a most shocking wartime experience that, although not itself common, was not at all unfamiliar to a watching Italian audience. Holland (2008: 548) indicates that he accessed the information through archive documents relating to the Resistance in Rome and the Lazio area at the Rome-based Institute for the History of Italy from Fascism to the Resistance (*Istituto Romano per la Storia d'Italia dal Fascismo alla Resistenza*). Lewis's celebrated wartime diary also contains additional details directly relevant to Loren's role. He makes clear that the woman that he encountered was not mad, but that, as result of her experience, was completely ostracised by the community of her village, a fate, he says, 'that was in fact worse than death': he then narrates that the Moroccan soldiers responsible for the attack were thereafter reported to be 'roaming the surrounding countryside in several jeeps' (Lewis 2002: 131–2). Later, he learns from a 'reliable contact' that the local Camorra carried out an act of revenge for the soldiers' conduct by luring four random Moroccan soldiers to a brutal death at the hands of the local villagers (Lewis 2002: 134).

Questions of performance cannot however be fully understood without reference to Loren's stardom, and the meanings of the role as they would have registered with contemporary viewers. In Italy, the role of Cesira resonated closely with perceptions of the persona already long established for Loren. She was again playing a woman of the people (*una donna popolana*), but now in melodrama, not comedy. Reception of the film was tied to a strong desire to reclaim Loren from modifications to her image that, it was suggested, came about through her links with Hollywood, but this argument is deeply contradictory. On the one hand it was felt that she had been 'stolen' by Hollywood and that the process termed 'the Americanization of Sophia' had influenced her work in a decidedly negative way. Specifically it was argued that the Hollywood practice of casting her in ill-suited roles, in heavy make-up and ostentatious dress, had distanced her from her 'real' identity – Southern, Neapolitan, a woman of the people – in other words, the persona established prior to her American adventure. The suggestion that she should now shed the trappings of Hollywood and re-establish connections with that persona was translated literally into the process enacted onscreen as, garbed in ragged dress, dishevelled and dirty, she is proposed as the antithesis of the Hollywood star.[14] On the other hand, one can say that these views are contradicted by the continued importance of the American venture as an essential part of her allure. The shorthand for her career, coined in Italy when she first left for Hollywood, was the phrase '*da fumetto a Hollywood*' (literally 'from comic strip to Hollywood'), and this captured the fundamental point that now distinguished her from virtually all other stars, Italian and European, of the period: her negotiation of, and successful return from, Hollywood. Implicitly Hollywood success is suggested to be the ultimate prize, the pinnacle of any career. Progress from aspiring starlet of the photo-romances to Hollywood, was quite simply another version of the rags-to-riches tale that, however hackneyed, continues to inform all aspirations to media success, whether it be the route of Lana Turner's story, first spotted as a waitress in a Los Angeles bar, or that of the shapely girls at a Miss Italia contest hopeful, as Loren once was, of being set on the road to stardom. All logic demonstrated that the urge to bring Sophia back to her roots was completely at odds with the wealthy, glamorous lifestyle she now led, amply set out on many magazine pages. However, it appears it was an impulse sufficiently powerful to allow for these contradictions to co-exist within a single persona. In this respect the shot of Cesira/Loren on the roadside played a role of considerable importance. It alone summarizes the film's claim to her seriousness as a performer, an image completely counter to the pin-up shots of Loren herself and many other shapely stars. Her body is on display but only as a huddled shape, bent low, in a pose that denies rather than proposes her body as the dominant spectacle.

Godzilla, Hercules and Sophia

The above heading gives a succinct summary of the rise of Embassy Pictures, a distribution and production company headed by Joe Levine, a self-made Boston film executive. Levine was responsible for the success of three films in the late 1950s, *Godzilla* (Honda, 1956) *Hercules/ Le fatiche di Ercole* (Francisci, 1958) and *Two Women*. While *Godzilla* and *Two Women* were classic examples of the so-called 'pick-up deals' (Guback 1969: 400), bought up only after initial production was complete, Embassy Pictures funded both production and distribution of *Hercules*, starring American strongman Steve Reeves. The film established a run of very successful peplum or sword-and-sandal films, many with Levine's support, that continued long into the 1960s. Following these early successes, Levine's involvement as distributor within the European film industry shows a diverse range of material from Fellini's 8½/*Otto e mezzo* (1963) to the films of Marco Ferreri, and Godard's *Contempt/Le Mépris* (1963).[15] The focus here is on the role of Embassy Pictures in the success of *Two Women* although, as Chapter 5 will show, the company was also to be involved in subsequent Loren films including *Boccaccio '70, Yesterday, Today and Tomorrow* and *Marriage Italian Style*. As far as one can ascertain from the budget documentation in the archive (ACS/PF/*Two Women*), Embassy Pictures had no direct involvement in the original funding of *Two Women*, but once distribution rights were established, Levine's stated aim was to promote Loren to success in the 1962 Oscars. He courted the media and spent substantial sums of money, very likely much more than the cost of the original distribution rights, in order to launch the film with a lavish premiere (Pryor: 1962); then, just as with *Hercules*, that opened simultaneously on 600 screens, he adopted an approach of 'blitzkrieg marketing' (Dale 1997: 32), taking out options with exhibitors to achieve what was termed 'saturation booking' (Maltby 1998: 34), and thus ensure strong returns for his investment. It was an enormously successful strategy that became the model almost two decades later for the launch of *Jaws* (Spielberg, 1975), the film credited with initiating the era of blockbusters in 1970s Hollywood (Maltby 1998: 34).

Levine, however, was not idly speculating on the earning power of a personality hitherto unknown: despite the limited success of her Paramount films, Loren retained considerable popularity with the US press and public. She was known for her films, but perhaps even more so as a 'personality', with appearances that capitalized on the potential of the nascent promotional route of television entertainment shows, in particular the popular Ed Murrow show *Person to Person* that ran on Friday evenings from 1953–9. A slot on this show, a fifteen-minute interview by Murrow of the chosen personality in his/her home, put her in the company of other personalities of the period as diverse as Jack Kennedy (and family), Fidel Castro, the Duke and Duchess of Windsor, and Frank Sinatra. The fact that 'Ed Murrow had invited you' was, it seems, sufficient to enhance the status of any personality (Persico 1988: 346) or, as Sperber expresses it, '*Person to Person* was a Friday night ritual, a kinsecopic record of an era, where participation came to be a status symbol' (Sperber 1986: 520). With its consistently high audience ratings, her TV interview with Murrow, broadcast on 11 March 1958, was probably seen by more viewers than had ever bought a ticket to see her US films. The fact that Murrow began his interview by informing his audience that 'Miss Loren has rented a suite at the Chateau Marmont, close to Sunset Boulevard and the Paramount studio' only enhanced the sense that she was a fully fledged Hollywood personality, echoed also in his comment, 'Well Sophia, you're almost one of us now' (Murrow: 2006).[16] She also made a guest appearance on the *Perry Como Show*, and with timing that was surely not coincidental to the forthcoming Academy Award decision, NBC ran a one-hour summary of 'The Life of Sophia Loren' in February 1962. Following Oscar success, ABC commissioned her, in an ambassador-type role, to present a documentary on the sights of Rome (Gould 1962 and 1964). Levine's career at this time was made possible by the increasing independence of distributors, as the implications of the separation of production, distribution and exhibition continued to impact on the US film industry. *Two Women* had its lavish premiere in New York in November 1961, and in the Maysles brothers' 1963 documentary *Showman*, film posters clearly visible on the screen have tellingly replaced the original opening credit 'Carlo Ponti presents ...' with the caption 'Joseph Levine presents ...'.

Levine is indeed the showman of this remarkable documentary that charts his career in the very period when he promoted Loren's films. It offers the most valuable insight into the work of Levine and the work of Loren and at the same time is highly entertaining, with its fly-on-the-wall style of presentation. The Maysles brothers were in this respect great innovators in the field, the acknowledged instigators of what became known as 'direct cinema' that in the same period was adopted also by documentarists such as Pennebaker and Gideon Bachman (Saunders 2007: 2). Shortly after *Showman* the brothers went on to make productions with a similar approach: a TV-screened documentary of the Beatles in 1964, *What's Happening! The Beatles in the USA*, and most famously their film on the Rolling Stones US tour, *Gimme Shelter* (1969). *Showman* contains extensive footage of Levine as he travels to Italy to present the Oscar statuette to Loren, who did not attend the ceremony. The original plan, to have Levine present it to her at the 1962 Cannes Film Festival, was vetoed by the Academy. Nevertheless, Levine ensures no photo opportunity for publicity from the waiting press is lost: we see shots of Levine's departure from New York, and arrival at Rome; shots of Loren with the statuette, Loren with Levine, Loren and Levine with the statuette; Carlo Ponti, Gustavo Lombardo and a host of other American and Italian executives are also regularly present providing supporting roles to the lead players so that it is not clear who gains most from the publicity – Levine, the Oscar or Loren. As we shall see in due course the deal struck for *Two Women* was the start of a long association between Levine, Ponti and De Sica, and at one point Levine is actually heard on camera saying to Loren, 'I bet you fifty dollars that next time I get you an Oscar for *Boccaccio* (sic)'.

Thus Embassy Pictures, and its promotional tactics played a major role in achieving success for Loren. How she was received in the film by American audiences is more difficult to judge. As Gledhill notes, audience reception of a film is a process of negotiation, and the factors that formed the basis of that negotiation were markedly different between an Italian and a US audience. As already noted, Italian audiences accessed the film largely through associations with Loren's work in popular cinema, but since the films of her early career remained unseen by many Americans the resonances of her role as Cesira were surely rather different for the separate audiences. The status of De Sica, and a renewed collaboration with Zavattini may have had additional bearing on the attention given to the film in America. Fellini suggested that in America at this time Italian films were generally able to draw on the 'aristocratic success' of Rossellini's *Paisà*, and De Sica's *Sciuscià* and *Bicycle Thieves*, but that as far as Americans were concerned 'there was no such thing as an Italian film industry, just those three films'(Farassino and Sanguineti 1996: 118). The tone is humorous, especially as Fellini's own films had enjoyed considerable US success in this specific period, but the point is well made. Irrespective of the actual content of Loren's film, it may be, initially at least, that exhibitors took screening options in the belief that they would recoup their outlay through the appeal of the established reputations of De Sica and Zavattini. Furthermore, Loren (and Lollobrigida before her) were generally viewed by international audiences as 'typically Italian', with nuances of the film's references to Southern locations much less apprehensible to a non-Italian viewer, for whom the specific wartime experiences would also have formed a more remote, unfamiliar spectacle. Loren's persona, as we saw in the welcome to Los Angeles in 1957, retained something of the quality of the traditional star; the film itself, as De Sica had suggested had an 'old-fashioned' air, thus retaining an appeal to traditional audiences that might well have contrasted with the draw of the so- called 'teen-melodramas' emerging in the same period in Hollywood. Finally, and not the least important, were the differing responses to the saga of Loren's marriage, where American onlookers, accustomed to much more lurid Hollywood 'scandals', assumed a perspective of amused detachment that doubtless engendered further sympathy for Loren's marital plight.

Loren's success in *Two Women* is attributable to many factors found in the different facets of her star status as manifested at national and international level. In recent times scholarly studies have focused on establishing and exploring the differing historical and social meanings audiences derive from cultural products (Gledhill 1999: 12), and the studies by Stacey (1994), Moseley (2003) and McLean (2004) are interesting cases in point. The issue is surely evidenced again in this study of the meanings 'Sophia Loren' carried for national and non-national audiences. While further study is required, especially as regards Loren's profile in the

Table 3: Box-office takings in Italy.

Film	Box-office takings	Annual position	Position in 1958–65
Two Women, 1960–61	L. 294,774,000	6th	54th
El Cid, 1961–62	L. 428,097,000:	3rd	20th
Boccaccio '70, 1961–62	L. 375,385,000	4th	25th
Yesterday, Today and Tomorrow, 1963–64	L. 675,200,000:	4th	4th
Marriage Italian Style, 1964–65	L. 939, 522,000:	2nd	2nd

Source: De Vincenti (2004), Storia del cinema italiano X 1960–64.

popular American press, the commercial impact of the film on Loren's (and not only Loren's) career is easily gauged, as box-office takings in Italy show in Table 3.

On this basis alone one can see that, rather than an isolated re-launch, the film served to trigger an increasingly lucrative run of box-office successes that cemented for Loren the status of leading box-office star in Italy, a monopoly position far divorced from the 'shapely star number two' label allotted to her on the eve of departure to Hollywood.

Notes

1. Some of the listed films belong to the category of popular 'episode films', that did not therefore require the commitment of a full-length film. The episode films included many comedies, but also auteur works such as We, the Women/Siamo donne (1953) and Love in the City/L'amore in citta (1953) that featured episodes contributed by directors such as Antonioni and Visconti. Loren's episode in A Slice of Life, entitled 'The Camera' lasts little more than five minutes: at 23 minutes, the rather longer 'Pizza Seller' episode in The Gold of Naples would still have required only a relatively brief shooting schedule for the individual participants.

2. The choice in any such listing of 'relevant films' is to an extent arbitrary. The list does not include other strands to the comic output such as OK Nerone (Soldati, 1951), My Son Nerone/Mio figlio Nerone (Steno, 1956) and Loren's own Two Nights with Cleopatra/Due notti con Cleopatra (Mattoli, 1953), a series of low-budget spoofs of the Hollywood biblical epics, largely because these eventually proved peripheral to Loren's main star trajectory. In addition, the contribution of Sordi and Totò to the comedy form is very considerable but would require a separate study, too extensive to include here.

3. De Sica's career as a comic actor, particularly the fortunes of the nice, eligible, young man (bravo ragazzo) of a range of 1930s films, is a major topic extensively covered in the publications by Snyder and Curle, and Cardullo that are listed in the bibliography. It is briefly noted here to clarify that when he returned to the screen in the 1950s, after his work as a director of neorealist films, the actor De Sica was not new to the comedy genre.

4. Margadonna is the main scriptwriters for the Bread and Love series, while Continenza was a major collaborator on the Blasetti comedy films. Brunetta (1998: 263–66) identifies the dominant figure

of the wider grouping as Cesare Zavattini, responsible for many of the great neorealist works, and notes also the centrality of Sergio Amidei. The names of Age and Scarpelli, and Steno are of significance largely to the comedy films, both as scriptwriters and also at times as directors. There are valuable individual interviews with many of these writers, and an overall assessment of the period, set out in the extensive study by Pintus, *Commedia all'italiana: parlano i protagonisti*.

5. My archive research was largely restricted to material that involved Loren and De Sica. Clearly there is a very long list of De Sica's comedy films in the 1950s and early 1960s that may reveal further detail on film authorship beyond what is officially entered under De Sica's name. Unfortunately the file on the first film of the *Bread and Love* series, *Bread, Love and Dreams* (Comencini, 1953) was unavailable, and may be located in another section of the State Archive. I have included the few references to the original film incorporated in later contracts. As far as the work with Loren is concerned, the documents are already extensive and, I believe, largely incontrovertible in the evidence they provide.

6. De Sica's first marriage to Giuditta Rissone produced a daughter, Emi. His second, long-term relationship with Mercader, with whom he had two sons Manuel and Christian, could not be formalized because of the absence of a divorce law in Italy. He and Mercader (like Loren and Ponti) took out French citizenship, and eventually married in Paris 1968.

7. As the naming *Pane amore e....* shows, Titanus eventually resolved to leave unfinished the Italian version of the film's title, despite the fact that they received an estimated 90,000 competition replies. This is sample evidence of the remarkable acumen of Lombardo, the studio head, who ran a number of similar publicity ventures in the 1950s with the specific aim of broadening the popular appeal of Titanus. In the same period he also ran a series of 'Titanus conferences' where the history of the studio, its budget, achievements and future projects, were periodically presented to the press and members of the industry (Bernardini and Martelli 1986: 142–44).

8. For a full listing of all awards, and those for Best Actress in *Two Women* (that include the national Silver Ribbon and Donatello David and the international successes at Cannes, the Oscars and the Hollywood Golden Globes) see Masi and Lancia (2001: 203).

9. The question of Loren's wider European fortunes is too extensive to cover fully here. For example her films were regularly dubbed into the German language and in West Germany throughout the 1960s she was regularly awarded the annual 'Bambi' prize as the year's most popular actress (Masi and Lancia 2001: 203). In a similar poll in Britain, taken soon after filming of *The Millionairess* she was voted as 'most popular female actress of the year'.

10. These are only examples of what became a lengthy history of Loren's association with a range of fashion designers. In the period we are considering, she was dressed by Balmain for the role of the heiress Epifania Pargena in *The Millionairess*, and the St Laurent connection was picked up again in the later *Arabesque* (Donen, 1966).

11. Further examples of Spinola's activities as press agent to a number of Italian personalities are found in his own highly amusing, colourful account in *C'era questo, c'era quello*; the period with Loren was a major aspect of his work, and is detailed very fully in the chapter 'Contro Sofia milioni di mamme' (Millions of mothers hostile to Sofia)' (pp. 40–54).

12. The most important of these was the fact that in the novel Cesira is much older, and in a detail impossible for the 25-year-old Loren to sustain, states that 'I developed a great affection for Michele, whom I came to look on as if he was my son' (Moravia 1957: 99). The film thus inevitably projects

the role of Cesira/Loren as instead much younger, with Michele proposed potentially as her lover, jealous of her attachment to Giovanni in Rome. This in turn also necessitated the casting of a much younger Rosetta (Eleonora Brown) from 'the voluptuous eighteen-year-old of the novel' to a 'prepubescent daughter' that modify substantially questions of the sexual charge present in the figures of mother and daughter (Marcus 1993: 77).

13. The planned shooting schedule and the actual shooting schedule as evidenced in the letters are broadly the same. The entire shoot, concluded in Rome, was completed slightly ahead of schedule. It required major *spostamenti*, cumbersome transfers of actors, crew and equipment that were often resisted, particularly by the technicians involved; latterly De Sica paints a picture of himself as 'the only one who really cares about the film', insistent on keeping to the original plan to use the locations he identified as suitable for the purposes of the film (*LS* 26 August: 77).

14. In making a connection with her Southern origins the Italian viewer will have been quite clear about the subtleties of difference between the Neapolitan strand – close to Loren's birthplace, an urban setting with marked local and culturally distinctive characteristics – and the identity of a woman native to the Ciocaria region (the meaning of the book's original title), defined rather in terms of a non-urban, peasant existence. As I suggest in the final arguments of the chapter, an American audience was likely to perceive it as an identity more simply, and broadly, Italian.

15. Remarkably, as in the case with Ponti , there appears to be no comprehensive study of Levine's career. Producers are of course less prominent in fronting a film's success, though this was hardly the case with Levine. The information in this section derives from two main sources: the Maysles Brothers documentary *Showman* (1964) and accounts of Levine's activities as and when they were reported in the *New York Times*. *Showman* is a treasure-trove of information both on Levine and Loren, who are presented in a remarkably informal style that was to become highly influential in future documentary filmmaking. It is not commercially available at present, and I am most grateful to the Maysles Brothers production company for making a copy of the material available to me.

16. The somewhat cloying tone apparent here in Murrow's interviewing was typical of the populist approach he took throughout the series, and was in marked contrast to the rigour of his role as a political reporter and investigator evident in his celebrated clashes with Senator McCarthy during the House Un-American Activities Committee (HUAC) trials of the early 1950s. Murrow defended this aspect of his work, saying that the very substantial sums he made from *Person to Person* gave him the freedom to carry out his other forms of journalistic activity. For further information on this see the relevant chapters in Joseph Persico, *Edward R. Murrow* (1988).

5

Loren and Mastroianni

The collaboration between Sophia Loren and Marcello Mastroianni is the most prolific on-screen partnership in the careers of both Loren, and of Mastroianni himself (Reich 2004: 105). They worked together almost entirely within the field of comedy. In the period 1950 to 1964, the focus of this study, they made five comedies together. Later collaborations included further comedies such as *The Priest's Wife/La moglie del prete* (Risi, 1971) and a 'reunion' film *Prêt-à-Porter* (Altman, 1994), but they also starred together in the melodramas *Sunflowers/I girasoli* (De Sica, 1971) and *A Special Day/Una giornata particolare* (Scola, 1976). Separately from his work with Loren, Mastroianni of course carved a wholly independent and highly successful career, but here we will focus on the relevance of Mastroianni to Loren's evolution as a star.

The early urban comedies
In this period Loren and Mastroianni made three films together that were, in order of production, *Too Bad She's Bad*, located in urban Rome and directed by Alessandro Blasetti, the rural comedy *The Miller's Beautiful Wife* (Risi), and *Lucky to be a Woman,* again directed by Blasetti and again using the setting of urban Rome. Additionally, Loren herself made one further urban comedy *The Sign of Venus* attributed to Risi but, as discussed in the previous chapter, in fact directed by De Sica. All the films belong to the classic period of pink neorealism, and fit its established subdivisions, the rural and the urban, that have been used an important point of reference for Loren's work. The early urban comedies of Loren and Mastroianni were produced by Documento Films that, as the name suggests, was set up in 1949 primarily as a documentary production company; in the early 1950s it was regularly contracted to make public information films for the De Gasperi government (Frabotta 2001: 52). The company sought to diversify by commissioning the Loren–Mastroianni films in the hope of emulating the success of the Titanus-based comedies (Cecchi D'Amico 2002: 196). Blasetti himself is clear on the importance of his role in inaugurating the Loren–Mastroianni partnership. He recounts that he had considered casting them together for the episode 'The Baby (*Il pupo*)' in *A Slice of Life* as a poverty-stricken couple who, in desperation, briefly abandon their baby in a Rome church: the roles were

eventually assigned to Mastroianni, with Lea Padovani as the mother, while Loren was restricted to appearing in the five-minute concluding episode 'The Camera'. As they worked together, however, Blasetti professed himself impressed by the way Loren 'held her own' against the improvisational technique of Totò (Figure 5), and this convinced him to assign her the leading role in *Too Bad She's Bad* (Faldini and Fofi 1979: 345). In contradiction to this, scriptwriter Suso Cecchi D'Amico claims that it was she and Flaiano who insisted on the casting of Loren as ideal for the very remarkable female lead they had created (Cecchi D'Amico 2002: 190). Either way, the role is interpreted as the film's greatest strength, a female figure 'completely new' to the film-making of the time (Grande 2003: 65); this is an argument that, as we shall see, is also relevant to the comic pairing as it plays out in the film. As in the rural comedies, the female takes the lead in the process of courtship, an aspect beautifully caught in the shot where Lina (Loren) lolls seductively against an astonished Paolo (Mastroianni) at the beach, but in contrast to associations with the rural, the urban setting gives an entirely different complexion to the gender roles. As Lina, Loren moves freely about the Rome metropolis and beyond, on a daytrip to the beach (Figure 6). Within the city she has few links to domestic space: her apartment home is effectively a safe haven where her 'father', Signor Stroppiani (played by De Sica), stores stolen goods and periodically leaves to carry out various scams on the city streets, ably abetted by his daughter. In this respect the film has been seen as a fore-runner to the various caper comedies such as *The Big Deal on Madonna Street/I soliti ignoti* (Comencini, 1958) that follow later in the decade (D'Amico 1995: 84). The father–daughter relationship has more of the semblance of a humorous rogue/accomplice combination, and Lina herself enacts a very independent role in public city spaces, parleying with the locals, arguing with policemen, and drawing Paolo, the ingenuous taxi-driver, into her web.

In contrast to Loren, Mastroianni was theatre-trained, affording him a more respected critical status than was evident in the disparaging attitude adopted towards the shapely stars of the period. However, he too served his apprenticeship in comedy, the same training ground as many other aspiring actors of the time. He had roles in a number of ensemble pieces, including an earlier casting as a taxi-driver in *Girls of the Spanish Steps/Le ragazze di Piazza di Spagna* (Emmer, 1952). By playing the part again in *Too Bad She's Bad* he was for a time concerned that he would remain forever type-cast in the role; nevertheless, he is adamant that this film with Loren was for him the major breakthrough to public popularity (Faldini and Fofi 1979: 345). Loren was thus the better-known figure, already with a major box-office success, *Aida* and *The Gold of Naples*, issued contemporaneously, that generated such intense press attention. If further proof were needed, one can see from the costings that she was paid considerably more than Mastroianni for both films, though in turn, both were paid much less than the older, more experienced male lead[1] (Appendix B, Archive Sample 4). To reinforce Mastroianni's lesser status his individual contract for *Lucky to be a Woman* specified that 'in the film's credits, your name will be in the same letter size, but in third place after the names of the other two main protagonists of the film' (ACS/CL/Mastroianni). Despite the evidence of the *Bread and Love* series, repeated use of a particular comedy couple was not standard practice in 1950s comedy films. More commonly the scripts were characterized by ensemble narratives of multiple courtships and rivalries, the roles of the heterosexual couples being continuously created, and just as quickly replaced both in terms of narrative (the roles themselves) and of casting (who

Figure 5: Alessandro Blasetti directs Sophia on the set of *A Slice of Life* (1953). Stills Department, Cineteca Nazionale, Rome.

Figure 6: Marcello Mastroianni and Sophia, the unruly woman on the beach in *Too Bad She's Bad* (1954). Stills Department, Cineteca

played the roles). Indeed the most regular comedy duo was in fact that of a priest and a communist mayor, namely Don Camillo and Peppone.

Giacovelli's analysis of the films of Blasetti at this time reinforces Grande's aforementioned point, that the role of Lina presents the viewer with a female figure 'completely new' to Italian film comedy. He argues that the films bear comparison not so much to other national comedies of the period, but rather to the work of Frank Capra and René Clair, an approach that offers valuable insight into the material (Giacovelli 1995: 36). Firstly, the structuring of the films, particularly in *Too Bad She's Bad*, differs radically from the standard formula of young woman/ young man/old man formula noted in the rural films with De Sica that is characteristic of the conventions of classical 'new comedy' (Frye 1957: 167). This substantially alters the dynamic of the courting couple, and draws the film-making closer to the conventions of screwball comedy that first emerged in 1930s Hollywood. Capra's 1934 film *It Happened One Night* is seen as a significant early example of the screwball tradition, which came to be characterized by a structure that eliminates the 'blocking' figure represented by the old man/father figure (Frye 1957: 169). It plays out roles proposing greater gender equality, resolved in a conclusion that asserts the social and sexual parity of the comedy couple. The scripting of both urban films envisages just such a gender relationship, as the male lead marks a decided departure from the colourless youthful partners of courtship in the rural comedies. Although still at a very early stage of his career, Mastroianni's role may nevertheless be read as laying claim to replace the old guard, particularly the powerful presence of De Sica; he tentatively takes over the mantle of the *bravo ragazzo*, the likeable rogue that De Sica had created in his 'white telephone' comedies of the 1930s. The referencing of Capra is also particularly relevant because *It Happened One Night* is explicitly cited in an international comedy success, Wyler's *Roman Holiday* (1952) that slightly pre-dated these films of Blasetti, produced as we have seen in 1954 and 1955. Although not fully cited in the credits, Suso Cecchi d'Amico and Ennio Flaiano had played a major part in scripting the Wyler film (D'Amico 2006); at the behest of Wyler, they carried out roles as script doctors of the film. The US scriptwriter was listed as Ben Hecht, but it is now clear that that Dalton Trumbo, one of the blacklisted 'Hollywood Ten', was in fact the true author of the original script.[2] With their work on *Roman Holiday* completed, Cecchi D'Amico and Flaiano now worked with Alessandro Continenza on the scripts for these early films featuring Loren and Mastroianni. *Roman Holiday* was one of a number of American runaway productions, that assigned a central significance to Rome, and more broadly Europe, within the cinematic culture of the period, as Nowell-Smith argues:

> After 1945 Europe has a new importance for America and for Hollywood. It is again Hollywood's biggest market. It is America's Cold War ally. A million GIs have come back from there, and millions more Americans will go there as tourists with the development of air travel. It also remains a site of fantasy, particularly sexual, and of old-country myths perpetuated by immigrants. (Nowell-Smith 1998: 138)

Thus, in the 1950s several international productions explored the cinematic and commercial potential of Europe as a site of fantasy. A wide-ranging analysis of the runaway productions in Spain notes that the Franco regime was initially reluctant to allow filming, but came to recognize the potential of cinema to encourage tourism from abroad that would thus bring economic and political advantage to an ostracized country (Rosendorf 2007: 78).

In Italy, several locations are used, though with Rome predominating in *Roman Holiday*, *Three Coins in the Fountain* (Negulesco, 1954) and the later *The Roman Spring of Mrs Stone* (Quintero, 1961) and *Light in the Piazza* (Green 1962). The setting of Venice serves a comparable function in *Summer Madness* (Lean, 1957), and one can also include Greece as presented in *Boy on a Dolphin* (Negulesco, 1957) with Loren herself, and *Never on a Sunday* (Dassin, 1960) with Melina Mercouri. Rossano Brazzi, an actor whose identity sits awkwardly between Italy and Hollywood, is frequently cast in these productions as the suave Italian suitor. As Reich has shown, it is precisely this stereotype of the Latin lover that Mastroianni consistently subverts in the roles he plays throughout his film-making career. In terms of the screen partnership of Loren and Mastroianni, a line can be traced from *Roman Holiday* to the Blasetti comedies and on to *La dolce vita* (1960), where Flaiano, now with a different group of collaborators, remained a major contributor to the script. The line of course connects the Hepburn-Peck roles of cynical journalist and (apparently) ingenuous young beauty to Loren and Mastroianni in *Lucky to Be a Woman*, and again to Mastroianni the world-weary journalist pursuing Silvia in *La dolce vita*. In different ways the Blasetti films may be understood as engaging satirically with

Figure 7: Marcello Mastroianni and Sophia, the unruly woman at the Colosseum in *Lucky to be a Woman*. Stills Department, Cineteca Nazionale, Rome.

the tourist view of Rome associated with the runaway productions. This is a perspective relevant also to Fellini's film, which in contrast offers a markedly more dystopian vision of the city. In Blasetti, the tone of the satire is less acerbic, as shown in a central sequence of *Too Bad She's Bad*. Lina (Loren) has a chance encounter near the Colosseum with two elderly tourists looking for directions and perhaps also a helpful, friendly guide to show them the city sights. In the taxi-ride that follows, to the complete bemusement of the passengers and Paolo the driver, Lina gives a running commentary in pidgin English, effectively a sly send-up of all gullible visitors, new to the city. The key shot immediately precedes the taxi-ride (Figure 7 and cover shot). Lina, busy ensnaring the timid Paolo, at first gives only scant attention to the tourists. She is momentarily framed in a shot with Paolo looking up at her, and the vista of the Colosseum fully displayed behind; as she casually leans back against a railing, the shot puts her on display as the glamorous indigenous city girl who, unlike Hepburn or Ekberg, is in natural alignment with the setting, fully cognisant of the possibilities that 1950s Rome might offer her.

The suggestion that, in the role of Loren, Rome has its own version of celebrity glamour is developed even more explicitly in *Lucky to Be a Woman*. The film opens with a scene showing a group of unidentified American stars arriving at Rome airport; they are greeted by a throng of excited press photographers, including the figure of Corrado, played by Mastroianni, and a curious public, including Antonietta (Loren) who begins the film as a simple shop assistant.[3] This opening airport sequence is replicated almost exactly in the arrival of Silvia (Ekberg) in Fellini's film later in the decade, but in this earlier version the focus is on a local girl, not a star being imported from outside. The celebrities are swept away in a waiting car, and the contrast is nicely set up between them and the star-struck working girl as she makes her own more mundane return to the city centre. As she does so she catches her stocking, bends over and raises her skirt to adjust it: the shot playfully recalls Ellie/Claudette Colbert's pose as she hitches her skirt (and a lift) in *It Happened One Night*. Antonietta's instinctive action to fix her stocking is fortuitously caught by the passing Corrado, himself on his way back from the airport with the photographers' posse. He transforms the shot into a voyeuristic, provocative pose that then, without her knowledge or consent, graces the cover of the magazine for which he works, accompanied by the caption 'caught posing on the Via Appia'. The shot of the girl unwittingly adjusting her stocking is thus changed into one that makes her a celebrity: with this cover, the process of transforming Antonietta into a leading fashion model begins. The editing cut from the out-of-town celebrities to Antonietta/Loren at first suggests a gulf between their glamorous lifestyle and the life of the homespun local girl. But as the narrative unfolds one can read the film as more boldly claiming, through Antonietta, that Italy now has its own glamour and its own stars who are not necessarily eclipsed by Hollywood. This links the argument of the film to the challenge European stars like Loren and Lollobrigida briefly made to Hollywood, discussed in an earlier chapter. It is a subject already hinted at in the episode 'The Camera' of Blasetti's earlier film, that opens with a cascade of fashion magazines, their titles (*Le ore, Epoca, La settimana INCOM*) clearly visible on the screen; this directly prefaces Totò's efforts to seduce Loren with promises that if she succumbs to his charms his camera can turn her into a glamorous cover girl. The theme was not uncommon in Italian films of the 1950s: it is seen in the narrative of Lisetta, the beauty contestant played by Lollobrigida in *Miss Italia* (Coletti, 1950), in Lucia Bose's aspiring model Marisa in *The Girls of the Spanish Steps*, and the eponymous role of

Donatella (Monicelli, 1956) played by Elsa Martinelli. As Buckley usefully observes the role of Donatella links Martinelli directly to Audrey Hepburn's transformation from Sabrina, unobserved daughter of a family servant to the elegant figure who returns from Paris to captivate both heirs to the family riches in Wilder's 1954 film (Buckley 2006: 327). However it is a topic that, with hindsight, clearly had particular resonance for Loren's future stardom.

The Hepburn–Loren–Ekberg lineage is marked by contrasts in their differing physicality, and the differing sexual charge of the roles they play. Since the cited films feature at an early stage in their careers (it was in fact Hepburn's debut film), they are important elements in establishing the star persona. Wyler told Cecchi d'Amico and Flaiano explicitly that in *Roman Holiday* he intended to create a protagonist completely different from the Italian shapely stars; for him Hepburn was to be a leading role with 'no arse, no tits, no tight-fitting clothes, no high heels. In short, a Martian. She will be a sensation' (D'Amico: 2006). Thus in the Blasetti films the curvaceous Loren reclaims the city for Italian film-making, an agenda that was in truth to be very short-lived. By the end of the decade Fellini's *La dolce vita* instead casts the voluptuous Ekberg, a figure of womanhood almost fantastical in its excess. Two years later, in 'The Temptations of Dr Antonio', the episode of *Boccaccio '70* directed by Fellini, the voluptuous Ekberg is again cast as a figure of allure, this time depicted as one that haunts the dreams (or better the nightmares) of Dr Antonio (Peppino De Filippo). But she exists only in exaggerated form, inflated to vast proportions on a giant poster located opposite Doctor Antonio's Rome apartment block, and visible every morning when he opens his blinds. She thus quite literally, and humorously, dominates not only his life but the entire district of the city where the enormous billboard is forever on display. Loren can be positioned between the two extremes of Hepburn and Ekberg, both in terms of her physicality, and the meanings of her role in the Blasetti films. As an emerging national figure in national film-making, she is closely linked to a city that does not, as in the case of the Hepburn and Ekberg, present itself as a location that is part-fantasy, to be visited and left behind. It suggests rather a place where the goals to which her particular character aspires (gender equality, social advancement, increased affluence) are representative of an emerging urban Italy and, as such, are accessible to all. Loren's physicality, initially so closely aligned to her Southern-ness, to the Naples area, is here proffered as central to the changing culture of mid-1950s Italy. Whereas in other pink neorealist films the meanings of gender relations are conveyed in coded form (Wood 2004: 136), here they are on the contrary quite explicit. Loren's roles invite associations with modernity, with youthful aspirations in an emerging, Rome-centred national discourse.

The status of actors in pink neorealism

This study has focused insistently on the importance of clarifying the place of the actor in 'the market of performance labour' (MacDonald 1998: 196), the 'market' of Loren's film-making in the 1950s. The box-office success of the urban films with Blasetti gave her a measure of success equal to the fortunes of the *Bread and Love* series, and one is thus tempted to consider the possibility that Blasetti had a degree of influence on Loren's early career comparable to that of De Sica. However, this analysis of Loren's career has also consistently challenged the perspective that as a star she was 'launched' or constructed through the influence of a single individual or group of individuals, and one can assert that the same argument holds true when applied to equivalent suggestions of 'launching' the comedy couple. The two films made by Loren and Mastroianni are more accurately described as simply a phase, though certainly an important one, of a longer series of urban comedy films directed by Blasetti that began in 1950 with *Father's Dilemma/Prima comunione*, continued with the episode films *In Olden Times* and *A Slice of Life* and beyond to *Love and Chatter/Amore e chiacchiere* (1958). Giacovelli (1995: 23) links them to what he categorizes as a major sub-genre of the period that he terms 'urban pink neorealism' (*rosa citttadino*) that both he and D'Amico (1985: 82) suggest should include the earlier, lesser-known trilogy of Luciano Emmer, *Paris is Always Paris/Parigi è sempre Parigi* (1951) the aforementioned *Girls of the Spanish Steps* (1952) and *High School/Terzo liceo* (1954), light comedies played out in various Rome locations.[4] It is particularly important to emphasize that this and similar productions with a Rome setting were filmed either before or contemporaneously with the classic rural comedies, of which the various *Bread and Love* films are such significant examples. There is a tendency to assume that the urban films followed chronologically, and evolved from the rural comedies: this in turn maps out a similar, and equally mistaken, trajectory for Loren's work, suggesting that she was launched first and foremost as Donna Sofia, and only later undertook roles that conveyed a more sophisticated profile. The evidence confirms rather that the Italian public instead accessed Loren through a body of comedy films, with rapidly alternating settings and appropriately alternating visual and associative characteristics. What is more, the urban comedies of Loren and Mastroianni must in turn be understood as part of the broader agenda of the period, marked by a rich vein of comedy, a form of popular entertainment that offered employment to a wide range of actors and technical practitioners: in this context, Loren and Mastroianni were important but at this stage not wholly exceptional figures. To approach the Blasetti films as 'star vehicles' built around a fledgling star couple would be to mis-read the particular conditions under which such films were made. One may reiterate the point that in this period only the films of Totò, and increasingly of Alberto Sordi, were devised around a particular star persona intended to showcase their distinctive, individual talents. For the majority of other actors, Loren and Mastroianni included, a steady stream of rapidly produced films is evident, and to a large extent casting was sought once the original 'idea' had been established, and perhaps even fully scripted. It is a method of operating summarized by Suso Cecchi D'Amico, one of the key scriptwriters of the time:

> In the early [postwar] period when we [Zavattini and I] worked together regularly, we went from one production company to another, offering our ideas for scripts for their consideration. At that time the situation in the industry was completely different: what happened was that the various producers asked us, the scriptwriters, to present them with narratives or ideas for narratives. They did not look to us to provide scripts devised for specific actors intended to promote them at the box office. (Cecchi D'Amico 2002: 82)

This is a tradition common to all genre film-making, found also in production arrangements for the classic genre films of 1940s Hollywood: in the so-called B-movies the process of casting functioned in a way that was quite different to arrangements to establish the star for the big-budget main feature, a practice played out in its most extreme form in the fevered hunt to find the female lead to play opposite Gable's Rhett Butler in *Gone with the Wind*

(Fleming, 1939). On the contrary casting was a secondary element in the development of the low-budget project that was the genre film. The formula, once established, constituted the central defining feature: the formulaic roles remained flexible and were not tied to a particular performer. Should it become clear that one actor would be unavailable for the scheduled shooting time, another could easily be contracted in. This did not preclude the possibility that a major star might emerge from within the field of genre film-making. Essential to the iconography of any genre is the visual coding by which the audience recognizes and instinctively classifies a particular film. It is conceivable that, through repeated casting, a particular actor becomes part of that iconography. His/her stardom may thus gather momentum from a particular genre form, but it remains nevertheless a by-product of genre film-making. The careers of John Wayne in the Western and Humphrey Bogart in gangster/noir films may be said to have evolved along these lines, and also to a degree in the fortunes of the shapely stars in the *Bread and Love* series. The formula role that Lollobrigida took on developed directly from Maria Fiore's part in the Castellani film: her role as Carmela is of the independent 'untamed girl' (*ragazza scatenata*) who in defiance of tradition of the conservative southern village and an authoritarian father, fights to wed her local sweetheart Antonio. Lollobrigida's remarkable success followed, and the role directly shaped the development of her star persona. As we have seen, subsequent contracts even allowed for a degree of personal input to the scripting. Though then abandoned by Lollobrigida, the part retained a quality of adaptability that meant it transferred almost seamlessly to Loren. One may even observe a continuation of this same role as the combative, independent female lead in the part played by Marisa Allasio in the cycle of *Poor But...* films towards the end of the decade, an argument to which we shall return later in the chapter. In initial scripting and casting, genre remains a form of film-making without stars: the emergence of a star persona is a facet that is subsidiary rather than essential to the process of genre production.

Lucky to be a Woman is the last comedy made by Loren before the Hollywood phase of her career began. Questions of how a partnership with Mastroianni might have evolved in the immediate aftermath of the success of the Blasetti films must therefore remain entirely speculative, but a few indications emerge that suggest their work together might well have remained a fairly brief encounter. Blasetti has been characterized as an inventive film-maker capable of quickly creating a trend within a particular genre form, only then to jettison it with equal rapidity (Giacovelli 1995: 36). His comedy films are indeed relatively small in number, and they show an abrupt shift-change from the melodramas of the 1940s such as *Four Steps in the Clouds/Quattro passi tra le nuvole* (1942) and the magnificent *Fabiola* (1949) that many see as the high point of his career.[5] Mastroianni moved immediately to further comedy work in *The Bigamist/Il bigamo* (Emmer, 1956) and *Summer Tales/Racconti d'estate* (Franciolini, 1958), before continuing to *The Big Deal on Madonna Street/I soliti ignoti*, the film that initiated a new phase of Italian comedy. He also made the first film of his arthouse career with a major role in *White Nights/Le notti bianche* (Visconti, 1957) reviving collaboration with Visconti with whom he had worked in theatre earlier in the decade. Arthouse productions continued to figure prominently both with Fellini, and the lead role opposite Jeanne Moreau in Antonioni's *The Night/La notte* (1960). Loren, it appears, was to take a separate route: Dino Risi reports that his work as director on *Poor But Handsome/Poveri ma belli* (1957) was originally set up as a Ponti production with

Loren, Walter Chiari and Ugo Tognazzi in the lead roles eventually taken by Marisa Allasio, Renato Salvatori and Maurizio Arena (Barlozetti 1980: 40). The film is itself significant not least because it was vaunted as a low-budget production, with a high degree of success that was repeated in *Poor But Beautiful/Povere ma belle* (Risi, 1958) and *Poor Millionaires/Poveri milionari* (Risi, 1959). Giacovelli (1995: 26) asserts that the box-office takings of these films saved the precarious finances of the Titanus studio (Appendix B Example 5). As we saw in Chapter 2, neither Titanus nor the Lux studio was to survive long beyond the end of the decade as mainstays of the industry.

This prompts the question, did Loren and Lollobrigida price themselves out of the Italian market? Or perhaps more accurately, did they conclude that the vagaries of the Italian film industry could never fulfil their aspirations to international earnings and success? It is fair to say that both actresses came to the same conclusion on the matter, as the figures in Appendix B show, but with very different career results. At the same time, however, the entire complexion of Italian comedy film-making was poised on the edge of a great transformation, and the reasons for this need investigation. At the simplest level, one might ask whether the departure of the individual shapely stars to a range of destinations (effectively leaving them unavailable for casting) – to Hollywood (Loren), to other film projects (Lollobrigida), to arthouse (Mangano) or to marital domesticity (Allasio) – was a contributory factor? Certainly Allasio, who married an Italian aristocrat, had no further involvement in film-making, and was absent from the cast of *Poor Millionaires/Poveri milionari* (Risi, 1959), the third and final film of the *Poor But...* series. Alternatively, given the advent of the economic boom, it can be argued rather that their initial signification as embodiment of the postwar revival had reached a point of inevitable decline. As we have seen in Loren's Hollywood career, the era of the pin-ups and their commercial viability had already come to a conclusion on the international front, and they were replaced by a diverse range of possible images of femininity from Kim Novak to Lee Remick, none of whom fully predominated on the screen. The same was true as regards European stars: the rebellious sexuality of a Bardot was more in keeping with the mood of late 1950s society, but the cool, bourgeois sophistication of Monica Vitti in the films of Antonioni, and of Catherine Deneuve in the films of Bunuel was also a strong presence in the cinema of the early 1960s. Either way, by the late 1950s Italian comedy offered younger actresses (Claudia Cardinale, Stefania Sandrelli) parts very much subordinate to the male leads (Mastroianni himself, Gassman, Tognazzi and Sordi) with clear implications for their on-screen and career prospects. Precisely why the 'anxieties of masculinity' (Gunsberg 2005: 93) proved to be such a dominant feature of the ensuing *commedia all'italiana* is a question explored by a number of critics. The change of emphasis was not restricted to film-making in Italy. In what is a close parallel with this profile of Italian film-making, German cinema also registered a 'dramatic shift' as Bergfelder notes:

> the most popular genres of 1950s [German cinema] had all but disappeared by the early 1960s, along with its most bankable indigenous stars. [...] The genres that emerged in the early 1960s marked a reorientation towards new audiences, away from the female and family constituencies of the previous period towards, particularly, male adolescents. (Bergfelder 2000: 147)

In Italy, the absence of more diversified information on audience statistics, by factors such as age, gender and social class, makes difficult a clearer understanding of the rationale for such changes in public preferences; but whatever the underlying reasons, from Loren's perspective, departure from Italian comedy film-making at this time certainly appears to have been a highly astute career move.

The Sign of Venus merits a place in this chapter because, although not part of the Loren-Mastroianni partnership, it resonates well with the Blasetti urban comedies in its innovative presentation of female identity and the city. The cast of this beautifully realized ensemble piece shows the wealth of talent that, at a price, Lombardo had assembled: Loren, Franca Valeri (who also wrote the script), De Sica, Alberto Sordi, Raf Vallone and support stalwarts Peppino de Filippo and Tina Pica (Figure 8). It is one of the very few films of the period that narrates fully the life of a working woman, the earnest but dowdy Cesira, a role that Valeri explicitly scripted for herself. The film's set designer Gastone Medin, who later worked also on *Two Women*, researched assiduously in the centre of Rome for a location suitable to depict the working life of the young clerk (Valeri). The interior office set, convincingly constructed, is consistently used

Figure 8: The 'usual suspects' of Italian comedy filmmaking in the 1950s: Sophia on the set of *The Sign of Venus* (1955) with (seated, from left to right): Raf Vallone; Sophia, Vittorio De Sica, Franca Valeri, (standing, from left to right): Alberto Sordi and Peppino De Filippo. Stills Department, Cineteca Nazionale, Rome.

as a focal point throughout the film, ensuring that her identity is tied directly to the urban working milieu. This is demonstrated again in the sequences showing her daily bus journey to the office, surely one of the few depictions of life as an Italian commuter. Loren's character, who plays Valeri's cousin Agnese, was added to the script at a later stage, and in a number of ways this enhances the range of the original idea (soggetto) of the film. In the opening sequence Valeri consults an astrologer who foretells that 'the sign of Venus' is in the ascendancy in her star chart and that this will ensure she is lucky in love. We then observe the diverging fortunes of the two women, Cesira and Agnese, as their romantic fortunes unfold. The film subtly and very cleverly undermines the idea that either woman is 'lucky' in the potential partners that come her way, nor indeed in the uncertainties of life in the evolving urban society where they play out their parts. Cesira, hard working and generous natured, pursues a number of men, each manifestly undeserving of her attention: the trickster Alessio (De Sica) who abandons her for a wealthy widow, Mario (De Filippo) who pursues Agnese and then grudgingly suggests he might take Cesira as a poor second, and Romolo (Sordi), a classic case of Italian-mother domination (mammismo), dependent on his mother for money and plagued by her anxious phone-calls demanding that he is safely home by midnight.

Agnese/Loren's love life at first serves as contrast to her cousin. She has to fight off her many admirers, and lands up with the good-hearted, handsome Ignazio (Vallone). But in another sense her fate is shown to be not so very different from the part that Valeri plays. The heady days of the romance are short-lived: pregnant, she and Ignazio now struggle to survive the limited possibilities the city offers a poor working-class couple. There are similarities to the episode of 'The Baby' of Blasetti's A Slice of Life but here the tone is much sharper, and the soft-centred or 'pink' (rosa) quality of the earlier film is replaced by a more bitter tone. This is particularly true of the conclusion to Valeri's narrative that closes with shots portraying her as ever-optimistic, preparing to continue her search for romance. The film has shown the emptiness of the prize that she seeks, that of traditional courtship and marriage; the narrative emphasizes the integrity of her character by repeatedly demonstrating the largely worthless nature of her masculine counterparts. With regard to Loren, absolutely the best moment in the film is found in the scene where she takes part in a job 'interview'. It quickly becomes clear that she cannot type, but this is of no real interest to her prospective boss, who proceeds to put a lecherous hand on her leg, occasioning her abrupt departure. The scene plays tellingly on the multiple meanings of Loren's persona, where she acts out in ironic manner the role of the supposedly empty-headed and unskilled cousin to Valeri's sharply competent city girl. It presents a most interesting interplay between on- and off-screen dimensions of her role that invites comparison with Monroe as Sugar Kane Kowalcyzk in Some Like it Hot (Wilder, 1959): both display a fine comic touch that challenges the reputation frequently given them as little more than pin-up performers. Rather than passive recipients of male attention, Monroe and Loren make explicit play on such over-simplifications, giving the lie to prevalent critical views that undervalue their very considerable skills as comic performers. Through an exploration of contemporary female identity achieved collectively by Valeri, Loren and the ensemble cast, The Sign of Venus investigates, without a trace of pink neorealist sentiment, the figure of the 'new woman' of urban Italian life that, as we have seen, was regrettably short-lived for Loren and the entire comedy tradition of the period.

The 1960s comedies

The early comedies of Loren and Mastroianni should not therefore be considered as star vehicles, but inasmuch as this is the case with the 1950s films, it will be clear that the opposite is true for the comedies that they filmed together in the 1960s, *Yesterday Today and Tomorrow* and *Marriage Italian Style*, both directed by De Sica. These films did indeed cast the actors as a star couple, and with great success. Theirs was by now an established stardom of sharply contrasting meanings that derived from the separate trajectories they had pursued in their careers, each very different in character. Questions of stardom inform both productions at many levels, on as well as off the screen, and this chapter will consider the subject by drawing largely on examples from their roles as Filumena Marturano and Don Domenico in the later film. However, before looking at the detail, a more general indication of the persona they had each established is necessary.

The stardom of Mastroianni

The role of Don Domenico in *Marriage Italian Style* had a particular logic for Mastroianni in that it echoed his roles in a number of other recent films, where he played the cuckolded or impotent male ultimately outwitted by a more wily female counterpart. Prior to the De Sica film he was cast in the eponymous lead in *Bell'Antonio/Il bell'Antonio* (Bolognini, 1960) and in Pietro Germi's *Divorce Italian Style/Divorzio all'italiana* (1962). However, Mastroianni's work was not restricted to the ambit of Italian comedy: his reputation as an actor, particularly at international level, was by now based at least as much on his roles in *La dolce vita* (1960) and *8½/Ottto e mezzo* (1963) as Fellini's urbane, disillusioned alter-ego. A further dimension that linked him strongly to European film-making was also developing at this time in his work with Marco Ferreri. As we have seen, his roles in Italian caper films such as *The Big Deal on Madonna Street* drew him into the masculine-orientated comedy in combination with Vittorio Gassman, Alberto Sordi and Totò. The savage, surreal quality of the Ferreri films already evident in *The Man with the Balloons/L'uomo dei cinque palloni* (1965) initiated a long association between Mastroiannni, this director and a wealth of European talent including Michel Piccoli, Philippe Noiret, Ugo Tognazzi and Catherine Denueve (Small 2007: 54). Thus Mastroianni's was a multi-faceted form of film-making, where he moved continuously between both Italian popular and arthouse traditions, and the wider spectrum of European film-making. The very marked diversity of his work becomes increasingly evident precisely in this period when he resumed his collaboration with Loren. It established him as fundamentally a different *type* of star to Loren with career moves that demonstrate a strong resistance to Hollywood orientation. This is turn results in a series of contradictions regarding their star status, where differences between critical and popular opinion, and between notions of Hollywood and European status become particularly relevant. Mastroianni was, without question, an actor of much greater range than Loren herself, but his standing is also shaped by the view, prevalent in critical quarters, that involvement in European film-making affords greater artistic prestige than Hollywood. One might be led to assume from this that, as a consequence, Mastroianni's output was less commercially successful than Loren's, but this is simply not the case. As we have seen, in commercial terms by the early 1960s Loren was the single most successful star in Italy, but whether in spite of or because of his diversified screen image, the films of Mastroianni had comparable box-office results. This is clear from the above selective listing of box-office returns for the separate and combined successes of the two stars. Details on the relevant distributors are included, and will be explored further in the section 'Sophia, Marcello and Joe Levine'.

It is of course debatable whether box-office ratings are a valid means of making critical assessment of an actor's career but if one accepts that, at least partly, stardom is predicated on the number of customers who buy a ticket to see particular films, then by this measure Mastroianni's was a star career of great success. Two points may be raised here to qualify the issue. Firstly, one may ask if it is accurate to consider Mastroianni as the star, the focal figure whose casting brought audiences to the cinema to see the films of Fellini. The fortunes of these films may be viewed instead as linked to the relatively brief period of European arthouse success on the national and international front, marked by the phenomenon of the director-as-star. Furthermore, in this case Fellini's is the gregarious, expansive personality that is most prominent at various award ceremonies tied to the cited films: at Cannes, where in the 60s he had 'a veritable love affair' with the festival (Corless and Darke 2007: 73), and in Los Angeles, where he travelled to attend personally a number of the Oscars ceremonies where his films had been nominated. The overall impression remains that it was Fellini, and the films themselves that took the limelight, with Mastroianni's well-known reluctance to court Hollywood popularity an additional significant factor (Philips and Vincendeau 2006). Fellini also figured repeatedly on the pages of the press, alongside shots of scandalous *paparazzi*-type events, such as Ekberg's comings and goings to Rome nightclubs, which became an integral part of his finished film. In different ways De Sica, Visconti and Antonioni were also considered the key figures both in terms of publicity and of critical appraisal in their many distinguished productions at this time. Secondly, one might attribute the supposedly scandalous, sensationalist content of films such as *La dolce vita* to be the element of greater bearing on the ratings rather than the marketability of its male lead. To a degree, this is true of Mastroianni's own run of 'satires on marriage' or *commedie anti-matrimoniali* (Giacovelli 1995: 93), that also fit what might be termed the 'scandal' category. The long gestation of the Fellini film served as a protracted period of pre-publicity that brought the expectations of the cinema-going public and the newspapers to fever pitch when it debuted at Cannes in 1960 (Corless and Darke 2007: 71).

Neither should one ignore the uproar in Southern Italy when *Divorce Italian style* was first screened, as a factor in the film's popularity. Protests about the film's representation of the mores of Southern society appear conversely to have influenced positively, and not unexpectedly, the desire of audiences to view this controversial account of troubled sexuality and vanity of the Southern Italian male. As we shall see, when looking to select material suitable for US distribution, Joe Levine sought to capitalize on such appeal in the films he purchased for US distribution. At the moment when he accepted the role as male lead in *Marriage Italian Style,* the stardom of Mastroianni can be characterized as combining a most interesting, almost contradictory blend of popular and arthouse elements, box-office success and arthouse prestige. His work and his persona articulate aspects of contemporary sexuality in the satirical films of Fellini and Germi in a style that was more immediately marketable and quite distinct from the treatment of similar themes in the contemporaneous films of Antonioni and Bergman. One of the most interesting aspects for this study is the contrasting perspectives adopted towards his career and the career of Loren. From inception, Mastroianni's is a career, first as a theatre actor, and then combining the popular and the arthouse, that was certain to be allotted a higher critical status. The reputation of Loren (and other shapely stars like Lollobrigida, Pampanini and Allasio) is forever marked by the fact that they came untrained to the profession. They are regularly termed as having been 'discovered', 'launched' and 'promoted', suggesting they were passive figures in a process that made them into stars. Mastroianni, on the other hand, is seen as one who shapes his career, chooses his roles, and actively defines his career path. The innate and very high quality of Mastroianni's skills is not in doubt, but there is certainly also evidence of certain prejudices that colour interpretations of female star careers. Even today, analysis of the career of a George Clooney will show marked and not dissimilar contrasts (active/independent/male vs passive/manufactured/female) to an equivalent profile of a Julia Roberts.

The stardom of Loren

Following *Two Women*, and prior to her casting anew with Mastroianni, Loren's career showed a very substantial continuation of that film's success. As Table 4 shows, subsequent films *El Cid* and the episode 'The Raffle (*La riffa*)' of *Boccaccio '70* took very high box-office revenues; but the critical and commercial failure of *The Sequestered of Altona/I sequestrati di Altona* (De Sica, 1962) made clear not even Loren's presence in the cast was a guarantee of success. The case of *El Cid* is particularly interesting because it revives the funding controversies noted in earlier runaway productions. Like *Legend of the Lost* it was heavily funded by an American major. Producer Sam Bronston in fact set up a full-scale permanent studio in Spain to shoot this and two

Table 4: Separate and combined box-office returns.

Film title	Release date	Box-office position	Distributor (US)
	(Italy/US)	Italy (1958–65)	
La dolce vita	3/02/60	10	Astor
Il bell'Antonio	4/03/60	n/a	Embassy
Two Women	21/12/60	54	Embassy
The Night	24/01/61	n/a	Lopert
Divorce Italian Style	20/12/61	17	Embassy
El Cid	21/12/61	20	Fox
Boccaccio '70	23/02/62	25	Embassy
The Sequestered of Altona	30/10/62	n/a	Fox
8½	14/02/63	40	Embassy
Yesterday, Today and Tomorrow	19/12/63	4	Embassy
Marriage Italian Style	17/12/64	2	Embassy

Sources: Bernardini (1993), *Il cinema sonoro 1930–1969*, Rome: Anica; De Vincenti (2004), *Storia del cinema italiano Volume X 1960–1964*, Venice and Rome: Marsilio/Bianco e Nero.

further major productions (Rosendorf 2007: 78); the casting alongside Charlton Heston, fresh from another hugely successful runaway production *Ben Hur* (Wyler, 1959), did no harm at all to Loren's popularity rating. As in the case of *Legend of the Lost*, the links tying *El Cid* to Italy were extremely tenuous, but like the earlier film the producers nevertheless succeeded in a bid for classification, and thus for funding, as an Italian national film, albeit at the level of 'minority status'. The information might again have remained buried in a government official's note, had it not been for the fact that the director Anthony Mann went public with the matter. In cases of 'minority Italian status', the classification for this particular film, the practice was to cite a ghost Italian producer (here a certain Giovanni Paoluccci) that supposedly justified the bid for national classification, but in this case Mann was not prepared to go along with the pretence. He viewed such a practice as harmful to his reputation and sued the film's producers for damages. As a major US director, an exponent of some of the very great Westerns of the 1950s, he was clearly not used to the refinements of European funding manoeuvres. The controversy triggered a revealing article sarcastically entitled 'Come si italianizza un film' that, to convey the underlying meaning, is best translated as 'How to get Italian government money for a non-Italian film production' (Anon (f) 1963). Shortly after, Mann and Loren worked together in another Bronston production, *The Fall of the Roman Empire,* but in this case without any financial input on the Italian front. The film was a commercial and financial failure that bankrupted Bronston, and was one of the last Roman Empire-type blockbusters (Richards 2008: 24). While there is still much debate about the value of the runaway productions to the European film industry, the fact was that after *Ben Hur* and *Cleopatra* (Mankewicz 1960), the emphasis and the monies had shifted definitively to Spain, and this was certainly not a positive development for the long-term prospects of the Italian film industry. Possibly the last example of this type of film on Italian soil was *Sodom and Gomorrah* (Aldrich, 1963), conceived as a joint venture between Lombardo at Titanus and Joe Levine of Embassy pictures, shot in Morocco and at Cinecittà. In a repeat of the fortunes of the Bronston film, production costs spiralled disastrously out of control. It was the final blow to the finances of Lombardo's studio that thereafter survived in a much curtailed form mainly as a distribution company. However for Loren, whose career would increasingly move away from Italy to transnational European productions, such concerns were of diminishing significance to her star career.

The casting of Loren and Mastroianni, the two leading Italian box-office stars, held out the promise of success to almost any joint venture they might undertake. One of the greatest difficulties of Loren's film-making was to identify a male lead capable of off-setting the powerful physicality of her screen presence. Mastroianni's comic roles present a very particular image of masculinity for Loren to play against. Reich defines the role type here as that of the *inetto* or anti-hero, at a loss (socially and sexually) to deal with an 'increasingly emancipated female character' (Reich 2004: 106). The problem, evident particularly in the roles of Loren's Hollywood career, was common to the work of many shapely stars, such as Marilyn Monroe, Ava Gardner, Rita Hayworth and Lollobrigida. In this respect Monroe is again perhaps the best example to cite: *The Seven Year Itch* (Wilder, 1955) casts her alongside an anodyne and little-known Tom Ewell, while her greatest comic success in *Some Like It Hot* is based on a triangular relationship with Tony Curtis and Jack Lemmon in full drag. The casting of Loren with Hollywood stars Anthony Perkins and Tab Hunter required the projection of an on-screen sexual dynamic as the central feature of films *Desire under the Elms*, with Perkins, and *That Kind of Woman*, with Hunter. Throughout the 1950s the popular press repeatedly promoted them and Rock Hudson in roles of assertive heterosexuality despite the fact that, at least in the case of Hudson, their identity as part of the Hollywood gay community was to become common knowledge. How such detail impacted on screen performance, and audience reception of the screen performance, is not easy to judge, but the potential to create an additional subtext to the films needs to be recognized. Once back in Italy, Loren's first main role in *Two Women* was a melodrama that, as we have seen, was carefully crafted and produced at a pivotal moment in her professional and private life. Intuitively or otherwise, it was perhaps understood (whether by Loren, Ponti, De Sica, Levine or in combination) that this particular form of success was unlikely to be repeated. Neither was a link to the innovative comedies of Rome re-established, but instead to Naples, thereby reviving a series of 'safe' roles, familiar from her cinematic past.

In *Marriage Italian Style* the actors' on-screen partnership is more interesting for the interplay of their separate personas than for the detail of the specific screen roles they enact. Ostensibly the humour of the entire film is predicated on a power struggle between an ageing Lothario and his fiercely independent mistress who is nevertheless subordinate to him in law, in her legal status (or, better, lack of legal status) within her partner's affluent enterprises. Although she has long been an essential part of his professional and personal life, she has no status in law. The film's narrative is driven by his decision to marry a young employee and abandon Filumena, and the battle of the sexes that ensues stems from her desire, not to ratify her own position but instead that of her three sons, one of whom, as she informs the astonished Don Domenico, is his son and potential heir. Questions of stardom create an additional level of meaning in the film: for the audience of the time, the screen presence of Loren and Mastroianni was the film's central defining feature and the separate types of stardom that they represented had a particular impact on how that audience responded to their roles in the film. It has already been argued that within popular (as opposed to critical) perception, 'Hollywood' stardom had secured for Loren a distinctive, monopoly position, that privileged her status as star over a 'European' equivalent; on this basis Loren's may fairly be judged to constitute the dominating presence in the film. In accepting a casting that implicitly placed him in subordination to Loren, Mastroianni reveals all the contradictions of the particular star persona that he cultivated (or was cultivated for him). Fresh from the critical success of some of the most acclaimed arthouse films of the period, he is clearly reluctant to be type-cast, and intent on maintaining diversity from the Fellini roles. However, the part of Don Domenico gives continuity to his earlier comedies with Bolognini and Germi. In performative terms Mastroianni repeats his rendering of Count Cefalù in *Divorce Italian Style*: the body language of Don Domenico is characterized by the same mannered demeanour, adopting again a sardonic mask with the same physical tics and curled lip. In *Divorce Italian Style* it remains unclear, almost to the last frame, which partner will triumph in the gender contest. But in *Marriage Italian Style* there is no such element of suspense: from the moment the film opens, and even before this, through the audience's preconceived estimation of the stars of the film, Loren's is the focal presence, while Mastroanni enacts, in self-deprecating fashion, a role that implicitly acknowledges her dominance as star. In this way their relative star personas operate in conflict to the suspense of the script as it derives from the original De Filippo play. The bitter tone of Filumena's tale, and the uncertainties about the outcome of her bid for legal respectability, is superseded by the fact that, irrespective of how the narrative positions them, it is Loren's stardom that definitively shapes the film's meaning.

The issue of subordination, in this case of Loren to the camera, was raised in the case study's analysis of *The Woman of the River*. In the reading of this earlier film it was debated whether Loren's body is fetishized, rendered passive by the framing of the shots or whether it was she who controlled the camera, using it as a tool to further her emerging stardom. In 1955, at that particular stage of her career, the answer was perhaps equivocal, but the issue emerges again with a different emphasis in relation to the films of the 1960s. The Raffle' episode of *Boccaccio '70* the body of Loren is the ultimate commodity to be purchased, the prize for the lucky man who buys the winning ticket. Equally, in *Yesterday, Today and Tomorrow* the striptease in front of Mastroianni offers varying possibilities of interpretation. Do we read it as a coarse exploitation of the Loren body devised to sustain box-office momentum (and gain another Oscar)? Or alternatively a tongue-in-cheek vaunting of that body by a super-star confident that she has control in deciding how it is displayed? The ambiguities of such performances remain, both for Loren and other pin-up stars, but the interpretation proposed for these films is that her stardom, now firmly established, runs counter to the positioning of her character on the screen, where she is thus only apparently subordinate to or attendant on male favour. The power of her stardom subverts the logic of her role in the on-screen narrative, thereby confirming her not as controlled but rather as the controlling presence in the films.

Sophia, Marcello and Joe Levine

In its production plans *Marriage Italian Style* displayed several elements already seen as significant in Loren's career. The film remains a vehicle for both stars, devised, cast and planned out, with the roles of Don Domenico and Filumena offering connections to the on-screen roles, and extra-textual personalities of both Loren and Mastroianni; but the film is also significant because of the forces at work to ensure its commercial fortunes. Like *Two Women*, Loren's films of the early 1960s were marketed and distributed in the United States by Joe Levine's Embassy Pictures. Despite the promise, heard on camera, Levine did not win another Oscar for Loren with *Boccaccio '70*; but the following year *Yesterday, Today and Tomorrow* did indeed win as Best Foreign Picture, a success greeted with some astonishment at the time. If one consults the listing of films distributed by Embassy Pictures Corporation, it is notable that a number of these films also secured nominations (though not ultimate success) for Italian cinema in the early 1960s, in particular Mastroianni for best actor in *Divorce Italian Style*. A full understanding of Levine's work as a promoter is yet to be achieved, and one of the greatest difficulties is certainly the absence or contradictory nature of the information surrounding his commercial activities. Throughout the 1960s he continued to woo the US industry, holding regular press conferences to announce his plans for several of the aforementioned films. However, the wording of the carefully devised press releases is always circumspect, stating that certain films are 'scheduled for production by Ponti and Levine' (Thompson 1963), but conveniently glossing over the precise details of the deal. As in the case of *Two Women*, the costings of both De Sica comedies (ACS/PF/*Yesterday, Today and Tomorrow* and *Marriage Italian Style*) show no input at all from Levine at the production stage. They were each formally registered as co-productions and, as Appendix B shows, all three films register budgets at a very similar level (Appendix B Sample 6). At what point Levine's monies entered the equation therefore remains unclear. It is well to remember Guback's comment that in international funding arrangements, the notion of a 'pick-up deal' left wide open how and when non-European funds might become part of the original financing plan (Guback 1976: 400). Corsi puts it another way when she says that American funding was notoriously difficult to trace because a range of strategies, 'whether legal or illegal', were used to get round restrictions in the movement of monies between the two countries (Corsi 2001: 69). Whatever the means employed, Levine's role remains of fundamental importance to the success of his own film company and, above all, to the careers of these stars.

This leads also to broader question of the influence of a distributor's choices in shaping audience tastes, particularly in the case of a US-based distributor selecting non-Hollywood material. It is a point still relevant to the contemporary film market, where the activities of maverick operators like the Weinstein brothers at Miramax were crucial to the success of films such as *Cinema Paradiso* (Tornatore, 1989) and *Mediterraneo* (Salvatores, 1992) and bear strong similarity to Levine's methods of operation (Small 2005: 24). De Sica himself has contributed to the debate by commenting that, 'I made too many films that depended on the will of American financiers. For example, I made a film with Sophia Loren that earned her an Oscar' (Samuels 1972: 28). Ten years previously De Sica had guided production of *The Gold of Naples* that was funded substantially by Paramount, in a deal under the terms of *compartecipazione* or American co-production, but there is no doubt that these 1960s comedies are of inferior quality to the earlier masterpiece. There is nevertheless a certain irony in the suggestion that US monies are in some way tainted – in contrast, one assumes, to some notion of the 'purity' of Italian or European monies. However, such opinions are not restricted to the personal view of De Sica, nor to the individual roles Levine or Ponti might have played in the process. In the case of these films, two points are clear-cut: both were released in dubbed form in the United States, and, exceptionally, *Marriage Italian Style* was released contemporaneously in Italy by Ponti's Italian-registered Champion and Concordia Films of Paris, and in the United States by Joe Levine's Embassy Pictures Corporation. To contextualize the matter further, it should be noted that throughout the early 1960s Embassy secured US rights for several films already discussed in this chapter. A summary of its distribution activities shows that in this period it handled material as diverse as *Divorce Italian Style*, *Il bell'Antonio* and *8½* while at the same time continuing with low-budget delights such as *Goliath and the Rebel Slave/Goliath e la schiava ribelle* (Caiano, 1963), *Hercules against Molock/Ercole contro Molock* (Ferroni, 1963) and *Maciste in King Solomon's Mines/Maciste nelle miniere di Salomone* (Regnoli, 1964). Levine's was in many ways an exceptional enterprise but Maltby (1998: 34) also cites the activities of American Independent Pictures (AIP) as a company that bought up distinctly B-movies, such as *Sinbad Against the Seven Saracens/Sinbad contro i sette Saraceni* (Salvi, 1964) and *Honeymoon Italian Style/Viaggio di nozze all'italiana* (Amendola, 1966), a film without Mastroianni in the cast, but echoing his film titles. Like Embassy, AIP was a company employing a strategy of saturation booking for these films (Dale 1997: 25). In a detail that links to the question of 'scandal' films, it is interesting to note that *La dolce vita* was first released in the United States in 1960 with subtitles by the arthouse outlet Astor Pictures but in 1965 AIP re-released it, this time in the dubbed format commonly used in its peplum films. Thus in the playlists of Embassy and AIP, arthouse and the popular met in a curious mélange, and one can only speculate on how the marketing policy of the two companies shaped perceptions of international audiences towards these very diverse films.

Critical and popular reception

It appears that only once did a Loren film, *Two Women*, find unanimity in its critical and popular reception. This is borne out if we consider the diverging responses for the 1960s comedies of Loren and Mastroianni. Whatever the fine points of funding, the general perception was that Levine's was the main influence in the production, and this came through as a particularly negative aspect in the general critical response that was distinctly hostile to the films. In the British press *Yesterday, Today and Tomorrow* was described as 'a film that will make a lot of money for Joseph E. Levine' (Sarne 1964: 29), while Italian critics were scathing about *Marriage Italian Style*, arguing that:

> This is a frivolous confection devised in what is called the 'Italian style' and suitable for satisfying the simple palates of a particular kind of transatlantic audience. Maybe we Italians can console ourselves by thinking of the advantages the film will have for our industry, given that it will certainly record very high takings at the box-office in Italy and abroad, but I would say that for us the cost is too high. (Micicché 1964)

More explicitly the critic of *L'Unità* on 20 December 1964 called it 'an over-blown pathetic spectacle devised to please transatlantic audiences', with an 'ugly' title that echoed the much superior *Divorce Italian Style*, and that was imposed on the film 'by its American co-producer Joe Levine'. However, in contrast to the largely localized distribution of their work of the 1950s, these Loren–Mastroianni films bucked the trend of 'inexportable' national comedies. US commentators were considerably more enthusiastic in their judgment. *Variety* (17 December 1964) considered it 'as clever a piece of picture-making as has come from abroad in many a day', while Crowther, who was unable to grasp the fine points of the earlier *Lucky to Be a Woman* was positively gushing in his observation that, 'When De Sica gets together with Loren something wonderful happens', and concluding that the film was 'an achievement that adds up to one of the dandiest films of the year' (Crowther, 1964). The films also garnered several international awards that showed them to be, in short, 'exportable'. At national level, there was a return to the pattern of how Loren's earlier output was received: approved and fêted by the general public, but less enthusiastically considered by the critics.

In many ways Loren's role as Filumena is a throwback – not to the sophisticated 1950s urban comedies, but to the Neapolitan, Donna-Sofia lineage of *The Gold of Naples*. As I have argued elsewhere, the source material for this Neapolitan strand is the theatre of Eduardo De Filippo and the short stories of Giuseppe Marotta, both marked by a deeply traditionalist, nostalgic view of the city (Small 2000: 203). Renato La Capria, the well-known Neapolitan writer, sees De Filippo's postwar writings as depicting ghost-like figures with little relevance to the contemporary world (La Capria 1988: 69), and critic John Gatt-Rutter (1996: 20) reinforces the point, suggesting that Marotta's stories, written in the late 1940s when he had already long since left his native city, depict a Neapolitan society that appears to be completely 'untouched by history' (Gatt-Rutter

1996: 20). The Neapolitan connection continued to be emphasized in international publications. For example, the *Life* edition of 11 August 1961 presented a six-page spread, 'Sophia goes back to her roots' where we see Loren pictured with an assortment of elderly Neapolitan relations in a humble Neapolitan setting. Reports of this nature use Naples as now little more than a convenient point of reference for Loren, with the accompanying 'family photos' engineered to reinforce a part of her persona that, as already noted, had long ceased to have relevance to her affluent, off-screen lifestyle. The actress's origins remained of course an important formative part of her image, but the implication of the article, that they were still a regular feature of her present lifestyle, has to be treated with some scepticism. Certainly in cinematic terms, Loren moved ever further away from film-making that was identifiably Italian: this was part of a more general shift in 1960s European cinema, away from genres based on recognizable national specificities towards 'cosmopolitan chase stories' (Bergfelder 2000: 147). The description immediately brings to mind her very successful role alongside Gregory Peck in *Arabesque* (Donen, 1966) later in the decade. It was a new direction for Loren that acknowledged the truth of Gina Lollobrigida's wistful comment, made some years later, that 'the great female roles of the past like *Bread, Love and Dreams* have not been available to me or to my younger fellow actresses for more than twenty years' (Faldini and Fofi 1979: 344).

Conclusion

The year 1964, and the comedies with Mastroianni may legitimately be taken to mark the conclusion to the most decisive phase of Sophia Loren's career. By then, irrespective of what might have transpired in her professional life, she was established as a star with characteristics that rendered her, in consumer parlance, a unique, one-off product. At this point even if she had, Garbo-like, completely withdrawn from the world of entertainment, her global reputation as the best-known screen figure of postwar Italian cinema would still have been assured. A summary of the intervening years right up to the present, can give only the flavour of what followed. Developments in the industry of the 1960s go some way to explaining the decline in the level of her screen appearances. In general Italian stars became less prominent in the wider film industry. Actresses Monica Vitti, Claudia Cardinale and Stefania Sandrelli sought, with a degree of success to sustain a career prominence at international level, but nationally, the prospects for even such skilled performers as these became increasingly limited. When Hollywood regrouped and gradually withdrew monies and productions from Europe *Variety* observed that, quite simply, the bottom fell out of the arthouse market (quoted in Balio 1998: 63). Furthermore, genre film-making, the mainstay of Loren's career, became progressively less national-specific (Bergfelder 2000: 147) and thus she, like others whose star persona was tied so closely to notions of national identity, was increasingly constrained in her choices of suitable screen material. We have seen that Loren's off-screen dimension always carried importance in shaping her status as star. In the late 1960s, this aspect came to dominate, and a series of events enabled her to reconcile her image with even the most traditional sectors of Italian public opinion (Gundle 1995: 380). Press interest in Loren increased, but as in the saga of her Mexican marriage even the most cynical commentator could not justify interpreting subsequent developments as remotely akin to a publicity stunt. Since the early 1960s Loren had embarked on a long and difficult path to give birth to her two children, Carlo Junior, born in 1968 and Eduardo, in 1973. In contrast to the difficult times of the late 1950s, these events were handled with an assurance gained from the high level of stardom she had now achieved. Even at this most personal time there is a strong sense, noted by Edith Head, in charge of costume at the Paramount studio, that Loren is the ultimate professional (Head 1960: 20).[6] Opportunities to turn events to her advantage in the press were not lost. While waiting in a Swiss clinic to give birth to her first son, Loren invited Secchiaroli, by now her personal photographer, to take photos that caught her on the balcony of her room in an advanced state of pregnancy. Together they devised a use of camera lens to give the photos a blurred quality, as if the shots were unauthorized (Bertelli and Secchiaroli 2003: 62). Copies of magazines that paid the appropriate sum to carry 'secret' shots of Sophia as mother-to-be flew off newspaper-stands and ensured the best possible rapport with the public, ever more transfixed as it awaited the event. We have seen that tactics like this had been a major part of Loren's strategy for some time, enabling her to sustain a high level of popularity with little recourse to efforts for screen success.

Perhaps inevitably, as with all older stars, her contribution to cinema is acknowledged in more recent times with 'lifetime awards', as well as brief but memorable appearances, such as the moment when she was summoned to open the Best Actor envelope at the Oscars of 1999 (a move none too subtle, given Roberto Benigni's candidature) with the ecstatic cry, 'Roberto!' But she continues to convey glamour and elegance in a number of ways. She featured as a model in the 2007 Pirelli calendar, and in the same year the press reported that she had promised to repeat her screen striptease if the Naples football team won the Italian League (they did not). Nationally her status remains curiously contradictory, though this is partly explained by the fact that she is domiciled elsewhere in Europe, and only occasionally visits her native country. Instead she travels frequently to the United States for business reasons, and to visit her son Eduardo, who is based in California. Following the death of Carlo Ponti in 2007, she has however set up an annual commemorative music festival that was inaugurated at Cortona, near Lake Trasimeno in summer 2008. The contradictions in her Italian status are clear from other events of recent years. In April 2006 several worthy groupings, on the initiative of the television presenter Vincenzo Mollica, duly mounted a very popular Loren retrospective at the Vittoriano Museum in Rome; but in October 2007 the same authorities forgot to issue an invitation to her to attend the first Rome Film Festival. At international level she is a genuine, and convenient, 'Italian icon' representing what is believed to be all things Italian. Loren herself contributes with good spirit to the humour linked to her persona. A greetings card is in circulation at present, presumably with her agreement, showing her as Mara the stripper in suspenders and a floppy hat with a caption from one of her most famous (and one suspects systematically modified) comments, 'Everything you see I owe to spaghetti'.

Cercando (still looking for) Sophia

This book has addressed fundamental questions of the nature of stardom and how it is achieved. The introduction noted that European stardom is a particularly neglected facet of critical analysis, and the impetus to find new ways to investigate the star-making process remains strong. The search to find the 'real' star persists in the tabloid press of today, but the star is of course a manufactured presence both on and off the screen. Understanding the diverse meanings of the star persona by surveying his/her reception in diverse audiences is one of the most recent developments. However, looking for any star, just as this book has 'looked for' Sophia, may also be validly carried out by surveying the documentation attendant on that career. Uncovering the relevant archive material is an important step, as this book has shown, a process that continues to be full of great potential. Such information is notoriously difficult to find, since the detail of many individual contracts are confidential and unavailable in the public domain. In a state-subsidized industry the converse is true, and this produces nothing short of a treasure trove of papers that enlighten our knowledge of a star career. The research of Neil Rosendorf on runaway productions in Spain, another government-subsidized industry in Europe, draws on similar documents in the Spanish State Archive, and demonstrates the very fruitful results that derive from this approach.[7] Cinema is an art form, but it is also an industry, and the star is an employee, certainly the most prominent, of those actively working in the industry. The meanings that build around a star image are rooted in the industrial processes that govern that industry, which in turn are a manifestation of the place cinema holds in a given culture. What is so interesting about Sophia Loren is the way her persona drew on and fused aspects of two separate but inter-related industries, of two separate but inter-related cultures, in Italy and in Hollywood, into a most spectacularly successful career.

Notes

1. For a fuller account of the costings of films and remuneration of individual actors, based on figures from the Central State Archive, see Appendix B.

2. See the account of the meetings between Wyler, Cecchi D'Amico and Flaiano by her son Masolino D'Amico, in D'Amico (2006) and his mother's own comments in Cecchi D'Amico (2002). She and Flaiano played the role of 'script doctors' for which she herself has said was a ridiculously low fee. Despite the fact that they virtually re-wrote the whole script Ben Hecht remained the official scriptwriter on the American credits, while she and Flaiano were acknowledged as contributing to the script only in European editions of the film (Cecchi D'Amico 2002:161). I would like to acknowledge the help of Robert Gordon of the University of Cambridge in alerting me to this information in a paper on the scripting of La dolce vita that he delivered at the SIS conference at Salford in July 2005.

3. Shots of international celebrities arriving at Rome airport were not merely a convenient cinematic invention. Instead, as the stars travelled to Italy to shoot the various runaway productions, their photos filled the popular magazines of the period. Photographers lined up at Ciampino airport and various Rome locations (the Via Veneto, the Hassler hotel, the nightclubs) to catch Gregory Peck, Ava Gardner, Tyrone Power and Orson Welles. The role of the paparazzi thus created a most interesting interaction between on- and off-screen celebrity status that became the subject matter of Fellini's film.

4. For informative accounts of pink neorealism that show the full range of films produced in the period see the section 'Ascesa e declino del neorealismo rosa', in Giacovelli (1995: 23–40) and the sections 'La fase bucolica' and 'L'Arcadia romanesca' in D'Amico (1985: 73–87).

5. For a fuller summary of Blasetti's long and at times contradictory career see Mario Verdone, Alesssandro Blasetti (Rome: Edilazio 2006). The view that in his comedy films Blasetti switched from 'a masterpiece, Fabiola to a trite form of filmmaking' is expressed by Suso Cecchi D'Amico (2002: 192). 'Scripting Fabiola was one of Cecchi D'Amico's first major commissions.'

6. As head of costume at Paramount, Head worked with many of the key stars of the period, and thus her opinion on Loren carries considerable weight. I am grateful to Reka Buckley for alerting me to the publication of Head's memoir. It is an opinion supported also by the comments of the eminent photographer Alfred Eisenstadt, who worked extensively with Life magazine in the 1960s, and did a

number of important photo-shoots with Loren. In a published retrospective of his career he stated that more than any other star personality, Loren was his favourite because of her 'complete professionalism' (Eisenstadt 1973: 56).

7. Rosendorf's work on the subject is clearly on-going. His most recent article builds on research activities since completing hi PhD in 2000. The information on aspects of Franco's approach to censorship and American film companies holds many parallels with the Italian film industry explored in this and other books. Rosendorf is at present writing a biography of film producer Samuel Bronson (Rosendorf 2007: 109).

REFERENCES

A note on sources and references

Where reference is made to 'box-office figures' the following sources are used:

Italian box office: I have used the data complied and set out by Barbara Corsi in the relevant volumes of the *Storia del cinema italiano* published by Marsilio and the Cineteca Nazionale and cited individually in the bibiography.

US box office: the task is more difficult and less accurate. In the 1950s and 1960s US exhibitors simply did not regularly supply this information. For Loren's films in the US I have relied on the annual figures published in *Motion Picture Herald* that provide the 'top box-office films' of the appropriate year. In contrast to the Italian box office information, the figures in this trade journal, part of the Quigley publications group, are decidedly limited. They are based on returns for both the United States and Canada; they list the successful films alphabetically, not in rank order of takings, and they are consistently presented without the relevant revenue figures. As noted in the main text, in the annual listing of the 'Top Films of...' by *Motion Picture Herald* only three Loren films are ever recorded for the period covered by this book: *The Pride and the Passion* in 1957, *Houseboat* in 1958, and *Two Women* in 1962. Making reference to this annual listing throws into relief some of the anomalies of Loren's US career, and highlights the fact that producers can never fully gauge nor secure profits from the vagaries of audience tastes. For example, the first big-budget film on Hollywood soil, *Desire under the Elms* is notable by its absence from the list; and although marketed with the same vigour by Joe Levine, the 1960s films with Loren and Mastroianni, *Yesterday Today and Tomorrow* and *Marriage Italian Style* do not repeat the very high box-office success of *Two Women*.

References to press materials use primary sources accessed as follows: for film reviews from *The New York Times* and *Variety* the collected volumes published by *The New York Times* and *Variety*, presented chronologically, are used. Reports on industry activities (regarding Paramount, Levine and Ponti and others) were accessed on the *New York Times* archive website. For *Variety* and *Photoplay* originals available on microfilm at the BFI library were used. The BFI also stores annual bound copies of *Motion*

Picture Herald and *The Film Daily Year Book* that were used for US audience and box-office information. Italian reviews of Loren films were generally accessed though cuttings in the individual film files of the Central State Archive. For the 'subsidiary literature' such as articles from *Gente, Vie nuove, Jours de France,* etc. the main source was the original press clippings of the Mina Fabbri collection. All other materials of this nature are cited individually as indicated at the appropriate point in the main text and in the bibliography.

Agnolotti, Braccio (ed.) (1956), 'Il capitale straniero nel cinema italiano', *Cinema nuovo* 10 March, pp. 135-7.

—— (ed.) (1953), 'Rispondono i produttori', *Cinema nuovo* 1 June, pp. 331-3.

Alden, Robert (1960), 'Hard sell for motion pictures: Joseph E. Levine spends huge amount to promote films', http://select.nytimes.com/gst/abstract.html?res=F40E1FF63E5916738DDDA00A94DD405B 808AF1D3&scp=1&sq=hard%20sell%20for%20motion%20pictures&st=cse, *New York Times* 29 May, accessed on 5 June 2007.

Alexander, Paul (1994), *James Dean: Boulevard of Broken Dreams*, London: Time Warner.

Amelio, Gianni (2007), 'Non voglio perderti' in Morreale (2007) pp. 11-24.

Anderson, Benedict (1983), *Imagined Communities: Reflections on the Origin and Spread of Nationalism*, London: Verso.

Anon (a) (1953), 'Lo scandalo dell curve', *Cinema nuovo* 1 March, p. 135.

Anon (b) (1957), 'Sophia Loren goes to Hollywood' and 'Italy's Box office bambina makes record deals in US', *Life*, 6 May, p. 1 and pp. 137-40.

Anon (c) (1955), 'Europe's no. 1 cover girl: Sophia Loren as fishmonger in new Italian film', *Life*, 22 August, p. 1 and pp. 42-5.

Anon (d) (1954), 'Report of the International Film Festival of Berlin 18-29 June 1954' (Pressburo, Berlin, nd).

Anon (e) (1959) 'La favolosa metamorfosi deall ragazza di Pozzuoli' *Oggi* 27th June 1959, pp. 34-7.

Anon (f) (1963): 'Come si italianizza un film', *Lo specchio settimanale di politica e di costume* 6: 34, 25 August.

Archerd, Armand (1957), 'Photoplay visits a movie set', *Photoplay*, 26 October, pp. 73-6.

Babington, Bruce and Peter Evans (1993), *Biblical epics: narrative in the Hollywood cinema*, Manchester: Manchester University Press.

Babington, Bruce (ed.) (2001), *British Stars and Stardom: From Alma Taylor to Sean Connery*, Manchester: Manchester University Press.

Balio, Tino (1998), 'The art film market in Hollywood', in Nowell-Smith (1996), pp. 63-73.

Barlozetti, Guido (1980), *Modi di produzione del cinema italiano: la Titanus*, Ancona: Di Giacomo.

Bazin, Andre (2000), 'De Sica: metteur en scene', in Curle and Snyder (2000), pp. 62-76.

Beauchamp, Cari and Henri Behar (eds) (1992), *Hollywood on the Riviera: The Inside Story of the Cannes Film Festival*, New York: William Morrow.

Bergfelder, Tim (2000), 'The nation vanishes: European co-productions and popular genre formulae in the 1950s and 1960s', in Hjort and Mackenzie (2002), pp. 139-52.

Bernardi, Sandro (2002), *Storia del cinema italiano 1954/1959 IX*, Venice and Rome: Marsilio/Bianco e Nero.

Bernardini, Aldo (ed.) (2000), *Cinema italiano 1930-1995: le imprese di produzione*, Rome: Anica.

—— (1993), *Il cinema sonoro 1930–1969*, Rome: Anica.

—— (1993), *Il cinema sonoro 1970–1990*, Rome: Anica.

—— (1993), *Il cinema sonoro 1930–1990: Indici*, Rome: Anica.

—— (1993), *Il cinema sonoro 1990–1995: Indici*, Rome: Anica.

Bernardini, Aldo and Vittorio Martinelli (1986), *La storia di Titanus: tutti i film*, Milan: Coliseum.

Bernardo, Aldo (2003), 'The actor's view: Marcello Mastroanni', in *Imago*, pp. 18–19.

Bertelli, Giovanna and Tazio Secchiaroli (2003), *Sophia Loren*, Milan: Rizzoli.

Bertellini, Giorgio (ed.) (2004), *The Cinema of Italy*, London: Wallflower.

Bizzarri, Libero, and L. Solaroli (1958), *L'industria cinematografica italiana*, Florence: Parenti.

Bravo, Anna (2003), *Il fotoromanzo*, Milan: Il Mulino.

Brunetta, Gian Piero (1999), *Storia del cinema mondiale: Vol. 1 Miti, luoghi, divi*, Turin: Einaudi.

—— (1998), *Storia del cinema italiano: dal neorealismo al miracolo economico 1945–1959*, Rome: Riuniti.

—— (1982), *Storia del cinema italiano dal 1945 agli anni ottanta*, Rome: Riuniti.

Bruno, Giuliana and Maria Nadotti (eds) (1988), *Off Screen: Women and Film in Italy*, London: Routledge.

Buckley, Reka (2008), 'Glamour and the Italian female film stars of the 1950s', *Historical Journal of Film, Radio and Television* 28: 3, pp. 267–89.

—— (2006), 'Elsa Martinelli: "Elsa Martinelli: Italy's Audrey Hepburn"', *Historical Journal of Film, Radio and Television* 20: 4, pp. 327–40.

—— (2003), 'The female star in 1950s Italy', unpublished PhD thesis, University of London.

—— (2000) 'National body: Gina Lollobrigida and the cult of the star in the 1950s', *Historical Journal of Film, Radio and Television* 20: 4, pp. 527–47.

Butler, Jeremy (1998), 'The star system and Hollywood', in Hill and Gibson, pp. 342–52.

—— (1991) *Star Texts: Image and Performance in Film and Television*, Detroit, Michigan: Wayne State University Press.

Callari, Francesco (1953), 'Che cosa si premia?', *Cinema*, 15 July, p. 5.

Cardullo, Bert (2002), *Vittorio De Sica: director, actor, screenwriter*, Jefferson, North Carolina, and London: McFarland.

Castello, Gian Luigi (1957), *Il divismo*, Rome: ERI.

Cavalli, Fabio (2007), 'Attori sulle barricate: gli anni della lotta per la dignità del lavoro artistico', Enrico Mara Salerno Archive http://www.enricomariasalerno.it/eventi_e_mostre_italia60.htm, accessed on March 25th.

Cheles, Luciano and Lucio Sponza (2001), *The Art of Persuasion: political communication in Italy from 1945 to the 1990s*, Manchester, Manchester University Press.

Chiarini, Luigi (1957), *Panorama del cinema contemporaneo 1954–57* Rome: Edizioni Bianco e Nero.

Chiti, Roberto and Poppi (eds) (1991), *Dizionario del cinema italiano: i registi*, Rome: Gremese.

Cigognetti, Luisa and Lorenza Servetti (1996), '"On her side": female images in Italian cinema and the popular press, 1945–1955' *Historical Journal of Film, Radio and Television* 16:4, pp. 555–63.

Cook, Pam (2001), 'The trouble with sex: Diana Dors and the blond bombshell phenomenon', in Babington (2001), pp. 166–78.

Cook, Pam and Philip Dodd (eds) (1998), *Women and Film: A Sight and Sound Reader*, London: BFI.

Corless, Kieron and Chris Darke (2007), *Cannes: Inside the World's Premier Film Festival*, London: Faber and Faber.

Corsi, Barbara (2002), 'La ripresa produttiva', in De Giusti (2002), pp. 143–61.

—— (2001), Con qualche dollaro in meno: Storia economica del cinema italiano, Rome: Riuniti

Cosulich, Callisto (2003), Storia del cinema italiano VII 1945–48, Venice and Rome: Marsilio/Bianco e Nero.

Crowther, Bosley (1964), review of Marriage Italian Style, New York Times, 21 December.

—— (1955), review of Too Bad She's Bad, New York Times, 12 April.

Curle, Howard and Stephen Snyder (2000), Vittorio De Sica: Contemporary Perspectives, Toronto: University of Toronto Press.

D'Agostini, Paolo (2007), 'Addio Ponti: l'uomo che creò Sophia', La repubblica, 11 January, pp. 48–9.

Dale, Martin (1997), The Movie Game: The Film Business in Britain, Europe and America, London: Cassell.

Damico, James (1991), 'Ingrid from Lorraine to Stromboli: Analyzing the public's perception of a film star', in Butler (1991), pp. 240–53.

D'Amico, Masolino (2006), 'On the scripting of Roman Holiday', http://www.mymovies.it/critica/persone/critica.asp?id=37004&a=4850, accessed on 3 August.

—— (1985), La commedia all'italiana, Milan: Mondadori.

D'Amico, Suso Cecchi (2002), Storie di cinema (e d'altro): raccontate a Margherita d'Amico, Milan: Bompiani.

De Berti, Raffaelle (2002), 'Il cinema fuori dello schermo', in De Giusti (2002), pp. 116–29.

De Cordova, Richard (1991), 'Genre and performance: An overview', in Butler (1991), pp. 115–24.

De Giusti, Luciano (2002), Storia del cinema italiano: Vol. 8 1948–53, Venice and Rome: Marsilio/Bianco e Nero.

De Laborderie, Renaud (1964), Sophia Loren, London: World Distributors.

Della Casa, Stefano (2003), Capitani coraggiosi: produttori italiani 1945–1975, Venice: Biennale di Venezia.

De Monte, Matteo (1956), 'Evitato a Cortina un incontro Sophia-Gina', Il messaggero, 31 January, p. 10.

De Santi, Gualtiero and Manuele De Sica (2002), Matrimonio all'italiana di Vittorio De Sica: testimonianze, interventi, sceneggiature, Rome: Associazione Amici Vittorio De Sica.

De Sica, Emi and Giancarlo Governi (eds) (1987), Lettere dal set, Milan, Sugarco.

De Vincenti, Gianni (2004), Storia del cinema italiano: Vol. 10 1960–64, Venice and Rome: Marsilio/Bianco e Nero.

Downing Lisa, and Sue Harris (2007), Catherine Deneuve: From Perversion to Purity, Manchester: Manchester University Press.

Drazin, Charles (2007), 'The French cinema and Hollywood: a study of two systems from the coming of sound to the collapse of the Production Code', University of London, unpublished PhD thesis.

Dyer, Richard (1993), Popular European Cinema, London and New York: Routledge.

—— (1998), Stars, London: BFI (first edition 1979, republished with a supplementary chapter by Paul Macdonald, 1998).

Eisenstadt, Alfred (1973), People, New York: Viking Press.

Ellis, John (1982), Visible Fictions: Cinema, Television, Video, London and New York: Routledge.

Ellwood, David (1999), 'Hollywood e la modernizazzione dell'Europa', in Brunetta (1999), pp. 823–34.

—— (1992), *Rebuilding Europe: Western Europe, America and Postwar Reconstruction*, London and New York: Longman.

—— (1985), *Italy 1943–1945*, Leicester: Leicester University Press.

Ellwood, David, P. and Gian Piero Brunetta (eds) (1991), *Hollywood in Europa: industria, politica, pubblico del cinema 1945–60*, Florence: La Nuova Italia.

Faldini, Franca and Goffredo Fofi (1981), *L'aventurosa storia del cinema italiano raccontata dai suoi protagonisti 1960–69*, Milan: Feltrinelli.

—— (1979), *L'avventurosa storia del cinema italiano raccontata dai suoi protagonisti 1935–59*, Milan: Feltrinelli.

Farassino, Alberto (1992), 'Il costo dei panni sporchi: note sul "modo di produzione" realista', in Zagarrio (1992), pp. 135–43.

Farassino, Alberto (ed.) (2000), *Lux Film*, Milan: Il Castoro/Fondazione Pesaro Nuovo Cinema Onlus.

Farassino, Alberto and Tatti Sanguineti (1984), *Lux Film: esthètique et système d'un studio italien*, Locarno: Festival de Locarno.

Forgacs, David (1989), 'The making and unmaking of neorealism in postwar Italy', in Hewitt (1989), pp. 51–66.

Forgacs, David and Robert Lumley (eds) (1996), *Italian Cultural Studies: An Introduction*, Oxford: Oxford University Press.

Fournal, Luc and Nicolas Tikhomioff (1960), 'Sophie la Parisienne', *Jours de France*, 2 January, pp. 28–34.

Frabotta, Maria Adelaide (2001), 'Government propaganda: Official newsreels and documentaries in the 1950s', in Cheles and Sponza (2001), pp. 49–61.

Frye, Northrop (1957), *Anatomy of Criticism: Four Essays*, Princeton, New Jersey: Princeton University Press.

Galt, Rosalind (2006), *The New European Cinema*, Columbia: Columbia University Press.

Gandin, Michele (1953), 'Fanno cinema guardandosi allo specchio', *Cinema nuovo*, 15 March, pp. 180–1.

Gatt-Rutter, John (1996), 'Liberation and literature: Naples 1944', *Journal of Modern Italian Studies* 1: 2, pp. 245–72.

Giacovelli, Enrico (1995), *La commedia all'italiana*, Rome: Gremese.

Girelli, Elisabetta (2009), *Beauty and the Beast: Italianness in British Cinema*, Bristol: Intellect.

—— (2004), 'Italian Identity in British Cinema', unpublished PhD thesis, University of London.

Gledhill, Christine (1985), *Stars and the Star System*, London and New York: Routledge.

—— (1999), 'Pleasurable negotiations', in Thornham (ed.) (1999), pp. 166–79.

Gomery, Douglas (2005), *The Hollywood Studio System: a history*, London: BFI.

Gould, Jack (1962), '"World of Sophia Loren" shown on NBC: Profile traces story of Italian film star', http://select.nytimes.com/gst/abstract.html?res=FB0F14F7345D177A93CAAB1789D85F468685 F9&scp=1&sq=%22world%20of%20sophia%20loren%22&st=cse, *New York Times*, 28 February, accessed on 5 June 2007.

—— (1964), 'Sophia Loren guides Roman tour: Eternal City the star of ABC program', http://select. nytimes.com/gst/abstract.html?res=F60811FB385E147A93C1A8178AD95F408685F9&scp=1&s q=%22Sophia%20Loren%20Guides%20Roman%20tour%22&st=cse, *New York Times*, 13 November, accessed on 3 June 2007.

Grande, Maurizio (2003), *La commedia all'italiana*, Rome: Bulzoni.

Gualino, Renato (1950), 'Le producteur, c'est (aussi) le créateur du film', first published as 'Il produttore è (anche) l'autore del film', in *L'Eco del cinema*, 3: 15 December 1950, translated and re-published in Farassino and Sanguineti (1984), pp. 242–47.

Guback, Thomas, 'Hollywood's international market', in Tino Balio (ed.) (1976), *The American Film Industry*, London and Wisconsin: University of Wisconsin Press, pp. 387–409.

—— (1969), *The International Film Industry*, Indiana: Indiana University Press.

Guidi, Guido (1959), 'Torno in Italia, magari in galera', *Retroset*, 5 June, pp. 22–3.

Gundle, Stephen (2007), *Bellissima: Feminine Beauty and the Idea of Italy,* New Haven and London: Yale University Press.

—— (2000), 'Saint Ingrid at the stake: Stardom and Scandal in the Bergman-Rossellini Collaboration' in Forgacs, David, Sarah Lutton and Geoffrey Nowell-Smith (eds), *Roberto Rossellini: Magician of the Real*, London: BFI, pp. 64–79.

—— (1999a), 'Feminine beauty, national identity and political conflict', *Contemporary European History* 8: 3, pp. 359–78.

—— (1999b), 'Il divismo nel cinema europeo', in Brunetta (1999), pp. 759–86.

—— (1996), 'Fame, film and the fashion system', in Forgacs and Lumley (eds) (1996), pp. 309–26.

—— (1995), 'Sophia Loren: Italian icon', *Historical Journal of Film, Radio and Television*, 15: 3, pp. 367–85.

Gunsberg, Maggie (2005), *Italian Cinema: Gender and Genre*, Basingstoke: Palgrave.

Hamblin, Dora Jane (1961), 'Lovely ways and wiles of Sophia Loren: che gioia la vita – what a joy is life!', *Life*, 11 August, pp. 36–42.

Harris, Warren (1998), *Sophia Loren: A Biography*, London: Simon and Schuster.

Haskell, Molly (1987), *From Reverence to Rape,* Chicago: University of Chicago Press.

Hawk, James (1955), review of *The Woman of the River*, *Variety*, 5th December 1955, 36.

Hayward, Susan (2004), *Simone Signoret: The Star as Cultural Sign*, New York and London: Continuum.

Head, Edith and Jane Kesner Ardmore (1960), *The Dress Doctor*, Kingswood, Surrey: Worldswork.

Hewitt, Nicholas (ed.) (1989), *The Culture of Reconstruction*, Basingstoke: Macmillan.

Hift, Fred (1957), 'Foreign stars "invade" US: Yanks love 'em if they know 'em', *Variety*, 3 April, p. 1 and p. 95.

Higson, Andrew (2000), 'The Limiting Imagination of National Cinema' in Hjirte and Mackenzie, pp. 63–73.

—— (1989), 'National cinema', in *Screen* 30:4 Winter 1989, pp. 36–47.

Higson, Andrew and Richard Maltby (eds) (1999), *'Film Europe' and 'Film America': Cinema Commerce and Cultural Exchange 1920–1939*, Exeter: University of Exeter Press.

Hjort, Mette and Scott Mackenzie (eds) (2000), *Cinema and Nation*, London: Routledge.

Hill, John and Pamela Church Gibson (eds) (1998), *The Oxford Guide to Film Studies*, Oxford: Oxford University Press.

Holland, James (2008), *Italy's Sorrow: A Year of War, 1944–45,* London: Harper Collins.

Hope, William (2005), *Italian Cinema: New Directions*, Peter Lang: Bern.

Hotchner, A. E. (1979), *Sophia Living and Loving: Her Own Story*, London: Michael Joseph.

Hudson, Dale (2006), 'Just play yourself, "Maggie Cheung": *Irma Vep*, rethinking transnational stardom and unthinking national cinemas', *Screen* 47: 2, pp. 231–32.

Kaplan, E. Ann (1983), *Women and Film: Both Sides of the Camera*, London and New York: Routledge.

Kashner, Sam and Jennifer MacNair (2002), *The Bad and the Beautiful*, New York: Norton.

Kendrick, Alexander (1970), *Prime Time: The Life of Edward R. Murrow*, London: Dent.

Kezich, Tullio and Alessandro Levantesi (2001), *Dino: De Laurentiis, la vita e i film*, Milan: Feltrinelli.

La Capria, Raffaele (1998), *Napolitan graffiti: come eravamo*, Milan: Rizzoli.

Landy, Marcia (2008), *Stardom, Italian Style: Screen Performance and Personality in Italian Cinema*, Bloomington and Indianapolis: Indian University Press.

—— (2000), *Italian Cinema*, Cambridge: Cambridge University Press.

Lewis, Jean (1958), 'Sophia: I have loved only once', *Photoplay*, January, pp. 23–7.

Lewis, Norman (2002), *Naples 1944: an intelligence officer in the Italian labyrinth*, first published 1978, re-issued and published by Eland.

Lollobrgida, Gina ((1953), 'Lettera a *Cinema*', 16 September, p. 3.

Loren, Sophia (1998), *Recipes and Memories*, Rome: Gremese.

—— (1984), *Women and Beauty*, London: Aurum Press.

Lucherini and Spinola (1984), *C'era questo, c'era quello*, Milan: 1984.

MacDonald, Paul (2005), *The Star System: Hollywood's Production of Popular Identities*, London: Wallflower.

—— (1998), 'Reconceptualising stardom', in Dyer (1998), pp. 175–200.

McDonough, Yona (ed.) (2002), *All the Available Light: A Marilyn Monroe Reader*, New York: Simon and Schuster.

McIntyre, Ellen (2000), 'In love and war: Vittorio De Sica's *Two Women*', in Curle and Snyder (2000), pp. 242–57.

McLean, Adrienne (2004), *Being Rita Hayworth: Labor, Identity and Hollywood Stardom*, New Brunswick, New Jersey and London: Rutgers University Press.

Malavasi, Luca (2004), *Mario Soldati*, Florence: Il Castoro.

Maltby, Richard (1998), '"Nobody knows everything": Post-classical historiographies and consolidated entertainment', in Neale and Smith (eds) (1998), pp. 21–44.

Marcus, Millicent (1993), *Filmmaking by the Book: Italian Cinema and Literary Adaptation*, Baltimore: John Hopkins Press, pp. 67–90.

—— (1986) *Italian Film in the Light of Neorealism*, Princeton: Princeton University Press.

Marinucci, Vinicio (1955), review of *The Woman of the River*, *Momento Sera* 1st December, p. 12.

Marotta, Giuseppe (2006), *L'oro di Napoli*, first published 1947; re-issued with an introduction and notes, Milan, Rizzoli.

—— (2004), *Le bellissime: Marilyn Monroe, Brigitte Bardot, Sophia Loren*, Rome and Naples: Avagliano.

—— (1959), 'Sofia: inchiesta sulle grandi del cinema', *L'europeo*, 2 August, pp. 16–21.

Masi, Stefano, 'Il divismo europeo degli anni sessanta', in Brunetta (1999), pp. 809–46.

Masi, Stefano and Enrico Lancia (2001), *Sophia Loren*, Rome: Gremese (first published 1984, revised and updated 2004).

Maysles, Albert and David Maysles (1970), *Gimme Shelter*, Maysles Films, New York.

—— (1964), *What's Happening! The Beatles in the USA*, Maysles Films, New York.

—— (1963), *Showman*, Maysles Films, New York.

Mercader, Maria (2002), 'Il denaro spegne l'immaginazione', www.desica.com/denaro, accessed on 26 July 2006.

Micicché, Lino (1964), review of *Marriage Italian Style*, Avanti, 21 December.

Mollica, Vincenzo and Alessandro Nicosia (2006), *Scicolone, Lazzaro, Loren*, Rome: Gangemi.

Monaco, Eitel (1958), 'Annual Report on the Italian Film Industry', in *Film Daily Yearbook*, New York: Quigley, pp. 616–18.

Moravia, Alberto (2006), *Anatomia di una stella: Alberto Moravia intervista Sophia Loren*, first published in L'europeo, 23 September 1962, republished in Mollica and Nicosia (2006), pp. 229–46.

—— (1957) *La ciociara*, Rome: Bompiani.

Mormorio, Diego (ed.) (1998), *Tazio Secchiaroli: dalla dolce vita ai miti del set*, Milan: Motta.

Morreale, Emiliano (ed.) (2007), *Gianni Amelio presenta lo schermo di carta: storia e storie dei cineromanzo*, Milan: Museo Nazionale del Cinema/Il Castoro.

Moscati, Italo (2005), *Sophia Loren: la storia dell'ultima diva*, Lindau: Turin, 2005.

Moseley, Rachel (ed.) (2005), *Fashioning Film Stars: Dress, Culture, Identity*, London: BFI.

—— (2003), *Growing Up with Audrey Hepburn: Text, Audience, Resonance*, Manchester: Manchester University Press.

Murrow, Edward (2006), 'Person to person interview with Sophia Loren', broadcast 18 March 1958, *Person to Person: The Interviews of Ed Murrow* DVD, CBS Broadcasting/ Koch Entertainment.

Neale, Steve and Murray Smith (eds) (1998), *Contemporary Hollywood Cinema*, London and New York: Routledge.

Nerenberg, Ellen (2004), 'La ciociara/Two Women', in Bertellini (2004), pp. 83–92.

New York Times collected film reviews (1970), Volume 4 (1953–58) and Volume 5 (1959–68), New York: Arno Press.

Nowell-Smith, Geoffrey (1998), 'The beautiful and the bad: Notes on some actorial stereotypes', in Nowell-Smith and Ricci (1998), pp. 135–41.

Nowell-Smith, Geoffrey with James Hay and Gianni Volpi (1996), *The Companion to Italian Cinema*, London: BFI.

Nowell-Smith, Geoffrey and Steven Ricci (eds) (1998), *Hollywood and Europe: Economics, Culture and National Identity*, London: BFI.

Osborne, Richard and Molly Haskell (2005), *Leading Ladies of the Studio Era*, Los Angeles: Turner Classic Movies.

Parigi, Stefania (1986), 'Intervista a Giuseppe De Santis', in Bernardini and Martinelli (1986), pp. 31–4.

Perriam, Stephen (2003), *Spanish Cinema and Masculinities in Spanish Cinema*, Oxford: Oxford University Press.

Persico, Joseph (1988), *Edward R. Murrow*, New York: McGraw-Hill.

Peverelli, Luciana, 'Notte a bordo del Sereno: Sofia sprizzava felicita', *Annabella* 24th May 1959, pp. 8–12.

Phillips, Alistair and Ginette Vincendeau (2006), *Journeys of Desire: European Actors in Hollywood*, London: BFI.

Pintus, Pietro (1995), *Commedia all'italiana: parlano i protagonisti*, Rome: Gangemi.

Price, James (2000), 'The case of De Sica', in Curle and Snyder (2000), pp. 210–19.

Pryor, Thomas (1959), 'Producers plan six pictures by '61: Ponti and Girosi will work with Paramount', *New York Times*, 6 February, www.newyorktimes, accessed on 3 June 2007.

—— (1957a), 'Hollywood dossier: Marlon Brando's plans – Sophia Loren lands', *New York Times*, 1 April, http://select.nytimes.com/gst/abstract.html?res=F10E1EFF395B12718DDDAD0994DC405 B8789F1D3&scp=1&sq=Hollywood%20Dossier%20-%20Marlon%20Brando%20plans%20-%20 Sophia%20Loren%20Lands&st=cse, accessed on 3 June 2007.

—— (1957b), 'Paramount plans two Loren films: Studio to co-produce with Ponti and Girosi', *New York Times*, 14 April, http://select.nytimes.com/gst/abstract.html?res=F70616FC355F11738DDDA80A9 4D8415B8789F1D3&scp=5&sq=Carlo%20Ponti%20and%20Marcello%20Girosi%20 Paramount%22%22&st=cse, accessed on 3 June 2007.

—— (1956), 'Hecht-Lancaster obtains two novels: Film company buys "Blaze of the Sun" and "Cry Tough" – Sophia Loren to star', *New York Times*, 12 January, http://select.nytimes.com/gst/abstract. html?res=F2091FF83459157B93C0A8178AD85F428585F9&scp=1&sq=%22Sophia%20 loren%20to%20star%22&st=cse, accessed 3 June 2007.

Quaglietti, Lorenzo (1980), *Storia economico-politica del cinema italiano 1945–1980*, Rome: Riuniti.

—— (1974), *Il cinema italiano del dopoguerra: esercizio, legge, distribuzione, produzione*, Pesaro: Mostra Internazionale del Nuovo Cinema: Quaderno Informativo No. 58.

Reich, Jacqueline (2004), *Beyond the Latin Lover: Marcello Mastroianni, Masculinity and Italian Cinema*, Bloomington and Indianapolis: Indiana University Press.

Richards, Jeffrey (2008), *Hollywood's Ancient Worlds*, London: Continuum.

Rondi, Gian Luigi (1998), *Un lungo viaggio: 50 anni di cinema italiano raccontati da un testimone*, Firenze: Le Monnier.

Rosendorf, Neal Moses (2007), '"Hollywood in Madrid": American film producers and the Franco regime, 1950–1970', *Historical Journal of Film, Radio and Television* 27: 1, pp. 77–109.

Ruffin, Valentina (2002), 'Totò al massimo', in De Giusti (2002), pp. 268–77.

Russo, Paolo (2004), 'La filmografia incompiuta di Giuseppe De Santis', unpublished PhD thesis, Rome: Università degli Studi Roma Tre.

Samuels, Charles (1972), *Encountering Directors: Interviews*, New York, Longman.

Sansa, Tito (1959), ''Torno in Italia col cuore in gola', *Oggi*, 23 July, pp. 10–13.

Sarne, Mike (1964), review of *Yesterday, Today and Tomorrow*, *Films and Filming*, Vol. 11: no.1 (October), pp. 29–30.

Saunders, Dave (2007), *Direct Cinema: Observational Documentary and the Politics of the Sixties*, London: Wallflower.

Schatz, Thomas (1981), *Hollywood Genres: Formulas, Filmmaking and the Studio System*, New York: McGraw-Hill.

Schumach, Murray (1957), 'Movie producer sells the public: Joseph E. Levine believes in extravagant openings', *New York Times*, 21 October, http://select.nytimes.com/gst/abstract.html?res=F50D14FF 3F5E147A93CBA9178AD95F458685F9&scp=1&sq=%22Movie%20producer%20sells%20 the%20public:%20Joseph%20E.%20Levine%22&st=cse, accessed on 5 June 2007.

Server, Lee (2006), *Ava Gardner*, London: Bloomsbury Press

Sheppard, Dick (1957), 'What has she got that Hollywood hasn't?', *Photoplay*, August, pp. 33–5 and 77–8.

Skolsky, Sidney (1957), 'That's Hollywood!', *Photoplay*, May, p. 24.

Small, Pauline (2007), 'Deneuve's Italian interludes', in Downing and Harris (2007), pp. 57–74.

—— (2005), 'Representing the female: Rural idylls, urban nightmares', in Hope (2005), pp. 151–74.

—— (2000), 'Constructing identity in Neapolitan cinema', *Journal of the Institute of Romance Studies* 8, pp. 195–210.

Sperber, A (1986), *Murrow: His Life and Times*, London: Michael Joseph.

Spoto, Donald (1990), *Stanley Kramer Filmmaker*, New York and London: Samuel French.

Spinazzola, Vittorio (1985), *Cinema e pubblico: lo spettacolo filmico in Italia 1945–1965*, Rome: Bulzoni.

Stacey, Jackie (1994), *Star Gazing: Hollywood Cinema and Female Spectatorship*, London and New York: Routledge.

Staiger, Janet (1985), 'The Hollywood mode of production 1930–60', in D. Bordwell, J. Staiger and K. Thompson, *The Classical Hollywood Cinema: Film Style and Mode of Production to 1960*, London and New York: Routledge, pp. 309–37.

Stern, Lesley and George Kouvaros (eds) (1999), *Falling for You: Essays on Cinema and Performance*, Sydney: Power Publications.

Street, Sarah (2000), *Transatlantic Crossings: British Feature Films in the USA*, London and New York: Continuum.

Tatti Sanguineti (ed.) (1999), *Italia Taglia*, Ancona: Editori Associati.

Thomson, David (2008), 'End of the affair: Why did we fall out of love with our film stars?', *Guardian 2*, 18 July, pp. 7–8.

Thompson, Kristin (1999), 'The rise and fall of film Europe', in Higson and Maltby (1999), pp. 56–81.

Thompson, Howard (1963), 'Four films scheduled by Ponti and Levine', *New York Times*, 17 January, http://select.nytimes.com/gst/abstract.html?res=FB0612FA3C581A7B93C5A8178AD85F478685 F9&scp=1&sq=Ponti%20and%20Levine&st=cse, accessed on 9 June 2007.

Thornham, Sue (ed.) (1999), *Feminist Film Theory: A Reader*, Edinburgh: Edinburgh University Press.

Variety collected film reviews (1983), Volume 9 (1953–8) and Volume 10 (1959–63), New York: Garland Publishing.

Verdone, Mario (2006), *Alesssandro Blasetti*, Rome: Edilazio.

Verlac, Pierre-Henri and Yan-Brice Dherbier (2008), *Sophia Loren: A Life in Pictures*, London: Pavilion Books.

Vincendeau, Ginette (2000), *Stars and Stardom in French Cinema*, London and New York: Continuum.

—— (1998), 'Issues in European cinema' in Hill and Gibson (1998), pp. 440–8.

Visentini, Gino (1960), 'Grande la Loren', *Giornale d'Italia*, 24 December.

Vitti, Antonio (1996), *Giuseppe De Santis and Postwar Italian Cinema*, Toronto and London: University of Toronto Press.

Wagstaff, Chris (1999), 'Il nuovo mercato del cinema', in Brunetta (1999), pp. 847–904.

—— (1998), 'Italian genre films in the world market', in Nowell-Smith and Ricci (1998), pp. 74–85.

—— (1995), 'Italy in the postwar international cinema market', in Christopher Duggan and Christopher Wagstaff (eds), *Italy in the Cold War: Politics, Culture and Society 1948–58*, Oxford: Berg, pp. 89–115.

—— (1992), 'A forkful of westerns: industry, audiences and the Italian western' in dyer and Vincendeau (1992), pp. 245–62.

—— (1989), 'The place of neorealism in Italian cinema from 1945 to 1954', in Hewitt (1989), pp. 67–87.

Wilkes, Ed (1957), 'Hollywood says: "Benvenuto, Sophia!"' *Photoplay*, July, pp. 17–19.

Willis, Andy (ed.) (2004), *Film Stars and Beyond*, Manchester: Manchester University Press.

Wilson, Elizabeth (1993), 'Audrey Hepburn: Fashion, film and the 50s', in Cook and Dodd (eds) (1993), pp. 36–40.

Wood, Mary P. (2005), *Italian Cinema*, London: Berg.

—— (2004), ' Pink neorealism and the rehearsal of gender roles', in P. Powrie (ed.) (2004), *The Trouble with Men: Masculinities in European and Hollywood Cinema*, London: Wallflower, pp. 134–43.

Woodward, Richard (2002), 'Iconomania: Sex, death, photography and the myth of Marilyn Monroe', in McDonough (2004), pp. 10–34.

Zagarrio, Vito (1992), *Dietro lo schermo*, Venice: Marsilio.

APPENDICES

Appendix A

The cinema documents of the Central State Archive (*Archivio Centrale dello Stato*) in Rome are extensively used in this book. It is thus important to establish a suitable referencing system for the various elements covered by the archive and cited in the text: they will be identified by abbreviations for the separate elements that make up the individual files as indicated in bold below. A brief summary of the rationale behind this material in the Central State Archive (ACS) is necessary so that the content of the files themselves is properly understood. The cinema files at the Central State Archive contain documentation as prescribed by Article 3 of the Andreotti Law of 1949. As Quaglietti (1974: 31) shows, the law stated that, in order to obtain state support for a film production, documents relating to the proposed production had to be sent to two groupings: to a department of the Banca Nazionale del Lavoro set up to deal exclusively with applications for cinema funding; and to a consultative committee of the Department of Entertainment and Tourism (*Dipartimento di Turismo e dello Spettacolo*) with the specific remit of judging the proposal and allocating the funds. Each proposal had to be accompanied by:

1. the film script (*scenaggiatura* **SC**)
2. the contract of hire (*contratto di noleggio* **CN**)
3. the summary of estimated costs (*preventivo finanziario* **PF**)
4. the shooting schedule (*piano di lavorazione* **PL**)
5. a list of the relevant technicians and actors

NOTE: This list is generally accompanied by copies of the individual contracts issued to actors and to the technical staff. In the latter case, set union rates applied to groups such as lighting and camera technicians, while more prominent roles such as director of photography, scriptwriters and costumes and set designers were contracted and paid on an individual basis. The contracts of the individual actors (*contratto di lavoro* **CL**), all separately negotiated, are also included. Files do not generally have a full complement of this documentation, but generally the contracts of the major leads are available. Where there is an element of the so-called 'compartecipazione' or American co-production (discussed in Chapter

Two), the contracts of the American artists, held by the participating American production company, are rarely available in the file

6. all correspondence relevant to the production, including negotiations regarding production and distribution with non-Italian companies (*materiali vari* **MV**)

NOTE: This final category is the most unpredictable in terms of content. In some files there is extensive additional correspondence, in others, none at all. Most files also include sample newspaper reviews of the film and other associated press reports (opening nights, festival and awards ceremonies, opinions of random spectators) but the criteria for selection of this material is not clear.

This process of application, established by the aforementioned law of 1949, exercised its influence on Italian filmmaking in two main ways. Firstly it was fundamental for producers, who were required to submit a proposed production for approval to merit its classification as an 'Italian national film', or a 'film of co-production status': if granted, this gave entitlement to the state subsidy and favourable system of loans operated by the film production section of the Banca Nazionale del Lavoro. Secondly, a point that is largely self-evident, it put in place a structure that gave government a very high degree of overview and control of the industry's activities, a subject widely discussed in Chapter Two of the main text. Thus for every film approved by the committee, there exists an individual documentary file. The committee was required to judge a film proposal on the vaguest of criteria, that it should be deemed of 'cultural merit' that conveniently left producers to divine what might meet the approval of a government-controlled body. A system of state subsidy operates in different forms in a number of European countries, and Dale gives a succinct summary of the relationship between producer and the awarding government committee:

> Subsidy committee members do not have either the time or the skills to properly evaluate scripts and therefore depend above all on direct acquaintance with the applicant, or personal recommendations. The judges are mainly concerned to know that the project has the right 'cultural' feel to it, and is not likely to ruffle any important feathers (Dale 1997: 229).

The files that make up the bid are held at the Archive at EUR, where the years 1949–1966 are fully catalogued. So, in contrast to industries funded by private concerns, the documentation of every film approved for funding by the committee has the status of a public document, and is available for public scrutiny. Referencing in this book uses a convention of ACS/documentation heading (estimated costs, shooting schedule, etc)/film title, or, in the case of an individual work contract the name of the individual actor.

Appendix B

In the main body of the text, reference is made to specific aspects of funding of particular films. It is worthwhile grouping these together, to offer a body of raw data that improves our understanding of Loren's career, and of the industry of the time. For a more comprehensive picture, it would be necessary to assemble a greater quantity of information. There is the potential to establish meaningful statistical detail of, for example, 'average duration of shooting schedule' or 'average remuneration for a lead actor'. In this section of the appendix are figures on Loren's work alone, with some comparable data on her contemporaries in the industry: it is also a snapshot that demonstrates what the potential might be for further exploration of the very rich range of information that this important archive contains. Any researcher would be naïve indeed to believe in the absolute accuracy of the figures found in the files: apart from any other considerations, the term 'preventivo' means just this, estimated costs, that were presented ahead of the actual and always unpredictable shooting process. Only very rarely does a file contain the details of the costing on completion (consuntivo); examples of this will be given, but it was clearly not a statutory requirement to submit this information. Some caution must therefore be exercised when considering the complete reliability of the figures quoted. For example, Barlozetti suggest that Titanus was one of several production companies to operate what we might now term 'creative accounting': setting up various separate companies to administer funding for a single film, a practice that may partly explain the proliferation of so many single-film entries in industry records. He states:

> In the 1950s and 1960s the films produced by Titanus are probably greater than can be accurately estimated. Like many other production companies, Titanus made use of a number of the so-called 'production companies of convenience' thus making it impossible for even the most conscientious researcher to track down fully the relevant figures. In our summary of their activities we have therefore restricted ourselves to relying on so-called 'official' figures, that is, data issued by Titanus itself (Barlozetti 1980: 232).

Archive Sample One: actors' contracts of the 1950s

From the files studied, references to a binding contract were found for a very limited number of actors as follows:

a) The file on *Jolanda, Daughter of the Black Corsair* (1954) contains individual contracts and record of payments to the following actors with the Ponti-De Laurentiis production company (in an overall budget of 122,885,000) :

May Britt Wilkins	2,500,000
Barbara Florian	2,400,000
Marc Lawrence	4,500,000
Renato Salvatori	3,000,000

Florian was later to appear in a number of Mario Bava film; Lawrence was a Hollywood actor blacklisted following the HUAC-McCarthy hearings of the early 1950s; Renato Salvatori progressed to another long-term contract, this time at Titanus, which, he says, 'greatly restricted my career prospects' (Barlozetti 1980: 46). In the estimated budget costs of *Two Women* he is again listed as being under contract, this time to Titanus. De Sica himself mentions this as a difficulty in shooting the scenes where the actor, as Florindo, was paid for only a week's work, which meant that shooting of his particular sequences had to be carried out under considerable time pressure (LS 13 October: 104).

b) The estimated budget of *The Gold of Naples* identifies Totò as 'under contract to Rosa Films'.
c) The estimated budget of *Poor but Beautiful* identifies Maris Allasio as 'under contract to Carlo Ponti Cinematografica'.

Archive Sample Two: two Ponti films of the mid-1950s

	The Woman of the River	The Ricefield
nulla osta granted	17/12/54	28/11/55
budget	384,450,000	430,000,000
filming schedule	July–November 1954	July–October 1955
first screened	29/12/54	26/12/55
earnings for female lead	20,000,000	25,000,000

Production company (both films): Excelsa/Ponti Cinematografica/Les Films du Centaur.

Bernardini in fact lists the Italian funding company of both films as Ponti-De Laurentiis/Excelsa, as his entries are based on the company under which the original application for funding was made. The relevant archive documents show a later hand-written amendment dated 19th April 1955 on the shooting schedule, after the film had been released, attributing Italian production to Ponti Cinematografica/Excelsa, and this is the production company also entered on the budget plan for *The Ricefield*.

Archive Sample Three: early Loren-Mastroianni films

Film title	Estimated budget	Individual earnings	
Too Bad She's Bad (1954)	197,000,000	Loren: Mastroianni: De Sica:	15,000,000 9,000,000 40,000,000
The Miller's Wife (1955)	470,000,000	Loren: De Sica: Mastroianni: Stoppa:	30,000,000 70,000,000 15,500,000 4,500,000
Lucky to be a Woman (1955)	370,000,000	Loren: Mastroianni: Boyer:	40,000,000 10,000,000 61,000,000

Archive Sample Four: the *Bread and Love* series

Film title	Estimated budget	Individual earnings	
Bread Love and Jealousy (1954)	357, 984,000	Lollobrigida:	30,000,000
		De Sica:	50,000,000
		Director:	14,000,000
		Merlin:	2,000,000
Scandal in Sorrento (1955)	570,000,000	Loren:	35,000,000
		De Sica:	93,000,000
		Risi:	6,000,000
		Cifariello:	5,500,000
		Carotenuto:	5,000,000
		Pica:	3,000,000

Archive Sample Five: Loren's major films of the early 1960s

Film title	Estimated budget	Individual earnings (lire)	
Two Women (1960)	605,700,000	Loren:	30,900,000
		Belmondo:	14,009,875
		Vallone:	3,090,000
		De Sica:	30,900,000
		Salvatori:	2,757,333
		Praturlon:	2,621,107
Boccaccio '70 (1962) No individual contracts available in the file	600,000,000	attori principali:	210,000,000
Yesterday Today and Tomorrow (1963)	695,000,000	Loren:	30,000,000
		Mastroianni:	44,000,000
		De Sica:	50,000,000
Marriage, Italian Style (1964)	650,000,000	Loren:	40,000,000
		Mastroianni:	50,000,000
		De Sica:	50,000,000
		Puglisi:	2,000,000
		Tecla:	1,500,000
		Praturlon:	1,352,700

Archive Sample Six: other comedy films of the 1950s

Film title	Estimated budget	Individual earnings	
Poor But Handsome (1957)	157,228,699	Allasio:	1,300,000
		Risi:	1,500,000
		Manni:	2,000,000
		Salvatori:	1,500,000
Actual budget expenditure (consuntivo)	187,111,257		
Beautiful but Poor (1958)	270,000,000	Main actors: (attori principali)	14,000,000
		Supporting actors: (attori secondari)	7,000,000

Individual contracts were not entered for the file of this film. Both Renato Salvatori and Alessandra Panaro are entered as 'actors contracted to Titanus', with varying monthly rates of pay. As we saw in Sample One, Salvatori's contract was still in place at the time of filming *Two Women*.

Film title	Estimated budget	Individual earnings	
The Sign of Venus (1955)	464,000,000	Loren:	20,000,000
		Vallone:	12,000,000
		De Filippo:	10,000,000
		De Sica:	8,000,000
		Risi:	4,500,000
		Rienzo:	3,000,000
		Pica:	2,000,000

Only partial provision of artists' contracts was available. De Sica's entry is clearly partial, with no record of payment for his participation as an actor in the film. Relative to his earnings in other equivalent films of the period, the sum stated – for his 'artistic input' (direzione artistica) – is remarkably low.

Archive Sample Seven: *Don Camillo* films of the 1950s

Film title	Estimated budget	Individual earnings	
Don Camillo (1952)	218,000,000	Fernandel:	27,000,000
		Cervi:	8,000,000
Actual Budget expenditure	442,370,000*		
Don Camillo's Last Round (1955)	453,466,000	attori principali:	118,000,000

*Guareschi, it appears, had regular contact with events on set, and the file is full of reports of anecdotes about his on-going involvement in the scripting process. One of the most interesting accounts is found in the documentation from the production company that applied for further government funding: in it they explain how the extra costs came about, for the following rather delightful reason:

> The initial costing was based on the initial scripting, which was extensively modified and amplified at the insistence of the author on whose writing the script was based, and these alterations were made with the agreement and support of the film's director and the co-producers. As a result, the initial estimated duration of the shoot was considerably extended with the consequent increase in costs for technical crew, actors' pay, and related personnel. In addition, it should be pointed out that during shooting the said author suggested that, to convey better the authentic atmosphere of the narrative, it would be necessary to add in sequences to include the participation of almost the whole population of the village where shooting was taking place.

An additional report in the file states that when shooting was complete, the whole village came out to take part in a party hosted by the filmmakers, to bid a fond farewell to cast and crew. For the second film of the series, Guareschi was again involved in discussion of the script: following a bizarre libel case involving the prime minister of the period, Alcide de Gasperi, the file reports show that correspondence was conducted with Guareschi imprisoned in nearby Parma.

Archive Sample Eight: Runaway productions (where Italy's status is classified as *minoritario*, generally signifying a commitment of 20% to overall costs)

Film/year	Budget	Earnings
Legend of the Lost/ 1957	1,135,553,230	31,500,000 (Loren) 155,000,000 (Wayne) 31,500,000 (Brazzi)
El Cid/1962	740,376,429	152,348,350 (Loren) 35,200,000 (Vallone)

Archive Sample Nine: films of the early 1950s made with Paramount funding

Film/year	Budget	Earnings
The Brigand Musolino/ 1952	273,645,000	15,000,000 (Nazzari) 15,000,000 (Mangano) 5,000,000 (Spadaro
The Gold of Naples/ 1954	566,387,000	45,000,000 (Toto) 10,000,000 (Loren)

Archive Sample Ten: films/earnings that serve as a comparison with Loren's work

Mastroianni

Film/year	Budget	Earnings	
Girls of the Spanish Steps/1952	92,595,300	650,000	(Mastroianni)
		5,000,000	(Bosé)
Bell'Antonio/1959	182,747,062	15,000,000	(Mastroianni)
		4,892,000	(Cardinale)
Dolce Vita/1960	786,407,419*	20,000,000	(Mastroianni)
		25,000,000	(Ekberg)
		2,350,000	(Gray)
		1,950,000	(Magali)
		850,000	(Aimée)
		850,000	(Barker)

* The file records the actual cost (consuntivo) as 877,324,980

Lollobrigida

Film/year	Budget	Earnings	
The Woman of Rome/1954	400,000,000	70,000,000	(Lollobrigida)
The Most Beautiful Woman in the World/1955	551,670,000	40,000,000	(Lollobrigida)
		14,000,000	(Gassman)
Imperial Venus/1963	1,500,600,000	50,000,000	(Lollobrigida)
		84,167,000	(Boyd)
		7,010,700	(Girotti)
		3,500,000	(Ferzetti)

Other

Film/year	Budget	Earnings	
The Belle of Rome/La bella di Roma/ 1955	220,600,000	34,000,000	(Pampanini)
		30,000,000	(Sordi)
		9,000,000	(Stoppa)

Films of the commedia all'italiana

Film/year	Budget	Earnings	
Big Deal on Madonna St/ 1958	207,198,410	10,000,000	(Mastroianni)
		10,000,000	(Gasssman)
		7,500,000	(Totò)
		6,000,000	(Salvatori)
The Great War/1959	472,798,541	20,147,000	(Gassman)
		17,510,000	(Sordi)
		10,000,000	(Mangano)

Film/year	Budget	Earnings
Il sorpasso/1961	298,000,000	84,000,000 (Attori principali e secondari)
A Difficult Life/1961	348,987,320	33,990,000 (Sordi) 8,415,400 (Massari) 3,917,112 (Fabrizi)
The Monsters/1963	301,303,070	14,805,560 (Gassman) 38,100,000 (Tognazzi) 2,422,350 (Merlini)